A GIRL'S GUIDE TO
fitting in fitness

First published in 2013 by Zest Books
35 Stillman Street, Suite 121, San Francisco, CA 94107
www.zestbooks.net
Created and produced by Zest Books, San Francisco, CA

© 2013 by Zest Books LLC

Typeset in Trade Gothic
Teen Nonfiction/Health & Daily Living/ Fitness & Exercise

Library of Congress Control Number: 2012943314

ISBN: 978-1-936976-30-0

CREDITS
EDITORIAL DIRECTOR/BOOK EDITOR: Daniel Harmon
CREATIVE DIRECTOR: Hallie Warshaw
ART DIRECTOR/COVER DESIGN: Tanya Napier
GRAPHIC DESIGN: Marissa Feind
MANAGING EDITOR: Pam McElroy
PRODUCTION EDITOR: Maija Tollefson

TEEN ADVISORS: Amelia Alvarez, Ema Barnes, Anna Livia Chen,
Huitzi Herrera-Sobal, and Felicity Massa

Manufactured in China
SCP 10 9 8 7 6 5 4 3 2 1
4500391198

A GIRL'S GUIDE TO
fitting in fitness

Erin Whitehead and Jennipher Walters

DEDICATION

This is for all of the teen girls out there. There's more to life than working out, but being active sure makes life more fun.

INTRODUCTION

When we first set out to write this book about teen fitness, we asked ourselves one question: "If we could go back in time, what would *we* want to tell ourselves back in high school about living a truly healthy lifestyle?" Turns out, we'd tell ourselves a lot—about eight chapters worth of goodies, in fact.

Right now, you may think working out and eating right are just about helping you look better in your swimsuit or improve your tennis swing, but the healthy habits you build now will have a huge impact on your life going forward.

From tennis and cheerleading practice to cooking healthy dinners with our families, we were lucky enough to grow up with pretty healthy role models for parents. However, even with that, we misstepped, trying a crash diet here and under-or over-exercising there. With all of the unhealthy messages out there to look and dress a certain way, it's easy to get caught up in the hype that you are your dress size or that a boy will never like you unless you can rock a string bikini. But, believe us, that's a bunch of hooey.

You are beautiful as you are, right in this moment. And you deserve to take care of yourself—to be healthy and strong and confident. Not because a celebrity selling a new kind of make-up tells you so, but because deep down you are worth taking care of. Not to be a certain weight, but to be your best and healthiest version of yourself.

As you flip through the pages of this book, you'll see we've shared our top tips on how to do just that. We've laid out a plan for you to easily and sanely fit fitness and healthy eats into every aspect of your everyday life.

In the first few chapters, we'll introduce you to all the fitness and health fundamentals you need to know. We'll help you with getting motivated and getting started, and teach you how to properly fuel your body for everyday life. Then after that, we'll get more specific with workouts you can fit into your already busy schedule, like a quick morning workout, a walking routine you can do after school, and a dance party that will get you sweating. Once you've gotten hooked on fitness, we'll show you how to pump up those workouts to get even more of a challenge! It's not all fitness either; we'll share our tips on eating better, busting stress, and getting plenty of recovery time, too!

Throughout the book, we investigate (and often expose) common fitness myths, share pitfalls to avoid, and highlight tips from real teens who have made fitness and health a priority. Be sure to check out our resources, too, which will give you tons of great websites for all of your fitness and health needs.

Whether you're hoping to *start* working out, or looking to take your fitness level up a notch, we'll help you get there. All we ask is that, in doing so, you pay attention to your body, and treat yourself with respect and love. For us, that was the missing piece to our teen-fitness puzzle: It took us too long to realize how awesome we already were!

So now, without further ado, let's get to it!

Table of Contents

CHAPTER 1

Why getting fit matters

You've heard it repeated a million times: You should eat right and work out. Diet and exercise, diet and exercise, diet and exercise. Simple, right? But between news of another new superfood and all the celebrity diet fads out there, it can get pretty confusing. And most people would rather watch a movie than spend their day munching on carrot sticks and sweating it out at the gym. Well, we're here to tell you that even though fitness can be a lot of work and take a lot of time, it doesn't *have* to. In fact, exercise can actually be enjoyable. (We swear!) Being just a little more fit can make you healthier, happier, and more confident—maybe even confident enough to ask that senior to the homecoming dance.

You don't have to do sit-ups for three hours a day or make a million trips to the gym to reap tons of feel-good benefits. There are a number of *little* changes you can make to your routine that will bring out your inner Jillian Michaels— starting today.

In the following pages, we're going to tell you everything we wish someone had told us back when we were teens. From avoiding the latest crash diet (been there, done that—sadly), to finishing the mile run in gym class without having a near-death experience, to valuing being healthy instead of just looking "skinny," we'll reveal the ins and outs of getting fit without sacrificing any of the other things that you already love to do. In fact, we've put together a chapter with get-healthy tips and tricks for each and every part of your day. We'll show you how to make a healthy breakfast, squeeze activity into your school day, unwind and de-stress at night, and even get your friends and family involved with your fitness efforts on a year-round basis. Each chapter also includes a sample workout, so that you can start getting fit today.

With just a few tweaks to your lifestyle, even the busiest of girls can be fit!

Real Teen TIP

Why I Work Out:

"I exercise to stay in shape and because it makes me feel better. I enjoy staying active because I have fun doing it."

— *Allie Vandeneberghe, 16, Junction City, Oregon*

WHY SHOULD I CARE?

Sure, fitness is definitely about looking good (and confidently wearing that swimsuit at the community pool), but it's also about feeling good. By adding just a little bit of activity here and there, you too can cash in on these five sweet benefits.

1. **You'll love the number on the scale.** Exercise has been proven to help with controlling weight—meaning that as the years tick by, working out as a healthy habit (and not as a dreaded chore) will help keep you at your healthy and happy best.

2. **Your mood will improve.** Ever heard of a runner's high, where you experience a rush after going for a jog? It's real, and almost all forms of physical activity—not just running—have been shown to boost mood and energy. So instead of relying on that energy drink to get you through study hall, try taking the long way back to your locker after lunch for an afternoon pick-me-up.

3. **It will make going to the doctor a breeze.** Getting at least 30 minutes of activity most days of the week is linked to lower cholesterol levels, better blood pressure, improved heart health, and a decreased likelihood of getting diabetes. While that may not mean a whole lot to you now, believe us, you'll be thrilled later!

4. **You'll improve your grades.** Research shows that active teens tend to study better, have better focus, and get better grades. Imagine how thrilled the 'rents will be when you bring home that improved report card!

5. **It can be fun.** The best part about exercise and the reason why it really matters is that once you find a couple of activities or exercises that you enjoy, it will stop feeling like a chore.

Whether you're practicing your dance moves or going for a walk around the neighborhood to get a break from your annoying little brother, fitness can be a really good time.

FINDING YOUR INNER MOTIVATION

When it comes to your health and fitness, *you* are the boss. Sure, your mom can encourage you to eat healthy meals, and a doctor can "prescribe" exercise, but you're the one who's in control, and you're the one who has the power to decide if you're going to grab fast-food on your way home or if you're going to take a jog around the track instead. Basically, no one can force you to do something you don't want to do. You have to find the desire to be healthy yourself.

So how do you find the motivation to add yet another item to your already packed to-do list?

It helps to focus on the benefits. Are you looking for more energy? A stronger body? Or do you just want more endurance at the school dance? Once you get started and begin to see a few of those benefits being realized, it will become that much easier for you to stay motivated for the long term. It also helps to realize that even little lifestyle changes and minor tweaks to your habits can have huge benefits over time. You don't have to overhaul your life or your schedule to fit in a little exercise or make healthier eating choices, and it doesn't take an hour-long workout every day to see results.

Before you get started, just know that nothing worthwhile is a quick fix. As much as you'd like to see instant results, you're not going to see rock-hard abs after a few days of doing sit-ups (although your abs might feel like a rock was thrown *at* them). But be confident that your body is changing inside and out, so stick with it. Trust us: Change is happening. Just like Rome wasn't built in a day, getting fit doesn't happen overnight!

How Exercise Makes Me Feel: Mad Libs Style

Favorite vegetable: _____
Favorite ice cream flavor: _____
Prized objects: _____
Favorite physical feature: _____
Favorite game: _____
Favorite animal: _____

Contrary to popular belief, exercise doesn't have to be as dull as an over-cooked _____ (favorite vegetable). In fact, it can be better than _____ (favorite ice cream flavor) ice cream, and more exciting than winning a mountain of _____ (prized objects). Its benefits are numerous, too. Exercise makes your heart healthier, and may even make your _____ (favorite physical feature) stronger. It can put you in a better mood, like winning at _____ (your favorite game). And after you start doing it a lot, you'll be as energetic as a(n) _____ (favorite animal). And seriously, who doesn't want to feel like a(n) _____ (favorite animal)?

❖ **Find the Right Motivation:** Never let someone else's clothing size or weight dictate where you think you should be. Everyone has a different body type, build, and bone structure. A weight that's healthy for your friend may be seriously unhealthy for you. So when you're setting a goal to get fit, be motivated by your need to be the best version of yourself, not someone else. Figure out a healthy weight that works for you—check with your doctor if you have concerns—and stick with that. And remember: Numbers never tell the whole story.

❖ **Pump Yourself Up:** Half of the battle of getting fit is finding the drive to do it. It may sound cheesy, but it's worth finding your own motivational mantra—something that's guaranteed to get you going. Nike's ever-popular "Just Do It" slogan is one of those basic yet effective sayings that can encourage you to keep pushing forward even when you'd rather quit. Something like "one step at a time" can serve as encouragement to get the ball rolling if you're feeling unmotivated. Even think about the songs that get you pumped, or the stories that inspire you, and try and come up with your own sort of mantra—something to get you out the door when you're struggling to get off the couch, and keep you moving when you want to quit.

While we're talking positivity, remember to avoid giving yourself a hard time. Avoid negative self-commentary. Talk to and encourage yourself as if you were talking to a friend. You'd never berate a friend for running slowly or needing a short rest during a workout (and with good reason!), so don't treat yourself any differently. Negativity won't get you anywhere, and positivity never hurts!

TRACKING YOUR PROGRESS

In the following chapters, we'll tell you all about the important parts of a workout program and share some actual workouts with you. Before you start, though, it's a good idea to step back and see where your fitness and health are now, so that you can pat yourself on the back as you tone up later.

❖ **It's Not All about the Numbers:** If you've ever watched any of those weight-loss reality shows on TV, you probably think that tracking your success is just about the number on the scale. But the scale is a tricky little monster. Your weight can easily fluctuate three to five pounds just depending on what you ate, when you went to the bathroom, and how much salt you've consumed. And getting fit often means gaining more muscle mass, and that's not a bad thing!

❖ **It's a Bad Idea to Wake Up and Let the Scale Determine Your Mood for the Day**. Do us a favor and weigh yourself once a week, not every day. It's the perfect balance of being aware of your weight without letting your weight rule your world. Remember, it's not about being skinny. It's about being healthy and feeling your best!

❖ **The Blech–Awesome Chart:** Instead of the scale, you can track your fitness based on how you feel. For example, the scale may not have moved, but you're fitting into your jeans better. Or you suddenly stopped falling asleep during calculus.

Take a second to rank yourself in the categories below from one to five—one being "blech" and five being "freaking awesome." It's important to do this before you start being more active so that you can see exactly how much better you're feeling after you start getting physical. Be sure to fill out the Wellness Tracker below every few weeks to see how being more active is improving your

Wellness Tracker Date:			
	Blech	Average	Awesome
Energy Level	1 2	3	4 5
Quality of Sleep	1 2	3	4 5
Stress Level	1 2	3	4 5
Confidence	1 2	3	4 5

Common Mistake: Focusing on What You Don't Like About Yourself

It seems every girl is guilty of focusing on her weaknesses from time to time. If you struggle to see your positive traits, take the time to list all of your strengths—on the outside and the inside—and refer back to them when you're feeling down and out. After graduation, people generally start to embrace individuality way more than they did in high school. So start celebrating your uniqueness now—even if it takes everyone else a few years to catch up!

day-to-day life as time goes on!

Have we sold you on fitness yet? Read on to Chapter 2 for the basics on how to get started with working out and having fun!

Basics of a fitness plan

Now that you know *why* it's important to get your workout on, let's get down to the question of exactly what it means to be fit. You might think that being fit means having six-pack abs or super-toned arms, but it's actually about much more than that. (How you look isn't a very good way to judge fitness at all!)

Just because someone appears to be healthy doesn't necessarily mean she's truly fit. True physical fitness comes down to three basic components: aerobic fitness, muscular fitness, and flexibility. Together, these three aspects combine to make your heart healthy, your skeletomuscular system strong, and your joints limber. Without these three things, it's darn near impossible to have a healthy and fully functioning body! All three of these can be measured to provide you with a quick and easy sense of where your fitness ranks at the outset. To test your aerobic fitness, take your heart rate for one minute both before and after you walk a mile. Also note how quickly you were able to walk. For strength, do as many push-ups (real or modified, where you have your knees on the ground) as you can. To test flexibility, see how far you can reach with your legs out in front of you. Be sure to record your "before" stats so you can see how much you progress over time!

To support the fitness trifecta of cardio, strength, and flexibility, you need to make sure that your weekly exercise routine includes all three of these essential pieces. It's not nearly as overwhelming as it may sound. We'll break it down bit by bit and tell you how to fit it all in, what to avoid, and how to track your progress! All of the workouts you need to get started are included in this book.

FIRST THINGS FIRST: THE WARM-UP

Warming up before a workout is a must! You want to slowly get your heart rate up and get your muscles moving—it's kind of like preheating the oven before you bake cookies. Doing so helps to prepare your body for exercise, which helps to decrease the risk of injury, improve your performance, and just make exercise feel better.

A proper warm-up should last anywhere from two to ten minutes, depending on how long your exercise session will last. If you're going out for a ten-minute power walk, a two-minute warm-up is fine. If you're about to play tennis for an hour, you'll want to dedicate ten minutes to warming up.

The whole point of a warm-up is to prepare your body for the specific movement you'll be doing. A good place to start is to walk or march in place for a few minutes. If you feel weird marching in place, gently move your body in the same ways you would in your actual workout. If you're about to play kickball, do some easy kicks, try some light jogging, and move your arms like you're pretending to throw a ball. If you're doing some weight lifting, walk in place for a few minutes to get your heart rate higher and then go through the motions of lifting weights—either using a lighter weight or using no weight at all.

You may think that a warm-up has to include stretching, but you actually don't need to do a lot of static stretching (like touching your toes). If you like stretching, feel free to hold your stretches for a few seconds, but no longer than that. The goal here is to loosen and lubricate your joints and move them through a full range of motion. That way, when it's time for your "real" workout to start, you're ready to rock it!

Once you've gotten those muscles warm, you're ready to get into the meat of your workout—cardio and strength!

Cardio

Aerobic activity, cardiovascular exercise, or just cardio—no matter what you call it, this portion of the exercise trifecta gets your heart pumping.

- **Why It's Necessary:** When you think of cardio, you probably think of your heart. And you're right—cardio's biggest benefit is strengthening the heart. But there is a ridiculous amount of benefits to adding cardio to your day. Cardio also improves your metabolism and can help you maintain or lose weight.

- **How to Do It:** Anything that gets your heart pumping counts as cardio. It can be as simple as walking quickly around the block or bumping it up to a jog or a run. Activities such as

swimming, biking, and jumping rope all count as cardio. So do sports like basketball, soccer, tennis, and hockey. Turning on your favorite radio station and dancing even counts as cardio. Just pick your favorite activity—or mix up a few throughout the week—and get moving!

So just how hard do you have to work? An easy way to see how much you're pushing yourself is by taking the "talk test." You should be able to talk, but not sing, while you're doing the activity. A "moderate-intensity" activity should do it—you'll be working hard enough to get your heart rate up, which will mean breathing will become a little more difficult. If you can hold a full conversation without

struggling for breath, then your intensity is too low—you're probably not working hard enough to get the best health benefit. If you're working so hard that you can barely get a word out, you're working at a "vigorous intensity," which may be too hard if you're a beginner. A moderate intensity, where you can speak a few words without having to take a breath, is right where you want to be! So push yourself enough for it to be a real challenge.

❖ **When to Do It:** The experts say that children and adolescents should aim for 60 minutes of physical activity per day. You're probably thinking, *Who has time for that?* Well, if those numbers seem intimidating, have no fear! You don't have to set aside tons of time each day to get your heart pumping. You'll gain health benefits even if you break it up into 10-minute chunks throughout the day—a walk to school, a short bike ride around the neighborhood after classes, and a 30-minute game of basketball in gym class would give you an hour of activity for the day.

❖ **Things to Avoid and Goals to Reach For:** When adding cardio (or any activity) to your routine, start slow! You definitely don't want to overdo it or get injured in the process. Don't go for a three-mile run your first time out, or try to beat an all-state basketball player. Instead, set smaller goals and build up over time. If you've never run before, start by alternating walking with jogging and gradually work up to a 30-minute run. Or if it's been years since you've been in the pool, do a few laps and then tread water for a while, taking breaks as needed.

❖ **How to Track Progress:** Watch your endurance and speed increase as you work cardio into your life. You'll be able to go faster and longer without feeling like you're working as hard. Physically, you'll notice that your lungs don't burn quite as much and you don't get winded as quickly. You'll be ready for that three-mile run in no time!

Strength

The weight room isn't just for boys anymore. Strength training is also important for girls of all ages!

❖ **Why It's Necessary:** Your muscles are meant to be used! Strength training helps to keep your body strong and fit by boosting your metabolism, making your bones stronger, improving your coordination, and even giving you more energy. In other words, having strong muscles makes anything physical easier! (Not to mention that muscles look pretty cool.) And we promise, you won't start looking like a heavyweight champ unless you're lifting ridiculously heavy weights for hours a day!

❖ **How to Do It:** You can build strength by lifting something heavy (like dumbbells or even soup cans or milk jugs!), pulling on resistance tubing, or even using your own bodyweight and gravity as resistance (think push-ups and squats).

An ideal strength workout uses every major part of your body: chest, back, arms, legs, butt, and core (your abs and midsection). For each exercise, you want to do 8 to 12 repetitions ("reps"). If you're a beginner, start off with one "set" of 8 to 12 reps. More experienced exercisers can do two or three sets.

Strength training challenges your muscles to work harder than they normally do. So if you can easily lift a weight 12 times without feeling challenged, grab some heavier weights! That way your muscles will build up over time, getting stronger and more efficient at just about any task you throw at 'em!

❖ **Things to Avoid and Goals to Reach For:** When doing any kind of strength training—especially weight lifting—it's important to have proper form. Keep your stomach firm to support your back, and keep your arms and legs slightly bent. Move through every exercise with a slow and controlled movement. When it comes to strength training, smooth is the way to go.

If you've never lifted before, start off without weights. Try moves like crunches, lunges, and push-ups, or, if you're feeling ambitious, lift dumbbells that are lighter. Five-pound dumbbells are a good place to start, but if that feels like too much at first, try three-pound dumbbells instead. As you get stronger, lift more! When doing any exercise, be sure to always listen to your body. It really does know best.

❖ **When to Do It:** You should do strength-building exercises two or three times a week, giving your muscles at least 24 hours of rest between strength sessions. There's no perfect time of day to work on your strength—whatever works for you is best!

- **How to Track Progress:** If you want to know how much stronger you're getting, track your progress in a journal. Log how much you're lifting—including reps and sets—and watch your strength grow!

Flexibility and Stretching

You don't need to be able to stretch into crazy contortions like the Cirque du Soleil performers, but a little bit of flexibility is important for your overall health and fitness.

- **Why It's Necessary:** Stretching not only makes you more flexible, but it also increases your range of motion and improves your circulation, which can help give you energy. Plus, it relaxes muscles that tighten up during workouts (which can provide real relief) and gives you the chance to wow your friends with your bendiness. Keep it limber, girl!

- **How to Do It:** Stretching should be the most relaxing part of your workout. Aim to stretch all of your major muscle groups, especially any focus areas from your workout. Hold a stretch

Ow, I'm Sore!

If you've ever gotten up in the morning the day after a tough workout and felt like you could barely move, you've experienced something called "Delayed Onset Muscle Soreness." Known as DOMS for short, this uncomfortable side effect of working out is actually your body telling you you're awesome! When you do an exercise for the first time or really push your body to work harder than it's used to, you create tiny microscopic tears in the muscle. Your body's systems then go in to repair these tears, making the muscle stronger, more efficient, and even a little larger. While you shouldn't push yourself so hard that you're sore after every sweat session, being sore every few weeks is a good sign that you're pushing yourself and getting stronger!

MYTH BUSTING!

"No Pain, No Gain."

Being tired and feeling the burn is one thing, but pain is another. If something doesn't feel right, or if your weights are so heavy that you have to compromise on form, stop. Also, if you ever feel a sharp pain or have pain that won't go away, it's important to see your doc.

for about ten seconds, release, and try again—aiming to go just a little deeper for a total of 30 seconds.

The good news is that flexibility training can be wrapped right into your workout. Both yoga and Pilates-type exercises will strengthen your muscles and increase your flexibility at the same time. Adding a yoga or Pilates session

to your week is a great way to get even more bendable.

❖ **When to Do It:** It's best to stretch your muscles after a workout, when they're warmed up. You'll get a deeper, more effective stretch that way. Plus, stretching feels the best after you've really pushed your muscles! Make your stretching routine the last leg of your cooldown, once your heart rate has come down a bit. Also, try to add stretching into your day while you're watching TV or doing homework. Even five minutes of stretching can help keep you limber. Besides, aren't you dying for a homework break every now and then?

❖ **Things to Avoid and Goals to Reach For:** Stretching, especially when you're just starting out, may feel slightly uncomfortable, but it should never be painful. If stretching hurts, stop doing that stretch! Use slow, fluid movements; don't throw yourself into the stretch, and don't bounce. Set goals for yourself along the way. If you're pretty bendy, try to bend just a little bit farther. If you've never been able to touch your toes, make that your (eventual) goal.

:• **How to Track Progress:** You'll be able to tell when your flexibility increases by how your stretches feel and by how much farther you can stretch. You might go from only being able to touch your knees to reaching past your toes. Stretches that were once uncomfortable will become a piece of cake. Or you might find yourself twisting into yoga positions you once thought were impossible. When your muscles start to feel looser and more limber, you'll know you're getting somewhere.

THE COOLDOWN

Once you finish that last lap or push out that last bicep curl, it's tempting to take your sweaty self right out of the gym. But you're not officially done with your workout until you cool down. Just as a warm-up eases you into exercise, a cooldown will slowly bring your heart rate back down and ease you out of the hard work and back to reality. Slow your pace down a few notches until you can

breathe a little easier before you stop completely. This may take just a minute or two, or it may take ten minutes. A good rule of thumb is to cool down for five minutes—but just listen to your body and you should get a clear sense of how much time you really need.

No matter what kind of workout you do, you should stretch your muscles afterward. Though some studies have shown that stretching doesn't reduce soreness after a workout, it will increase flexibility, and it's best to stretch those muscles when they're warm.

GETTING STARTED

You might think that fitting strength, cardio, and stretching into your already busy life would be tough, but we promise it's not! In the following chapters, we'll show you ways to fit all three into every part of your day and week. Whether it's squeezing a workout in before or after school, making time for extra fitness on the weekends, or adding a bit of activity here and there throughout your usual daily routine, you don't have to completely overhaul your schedule to get fit. When starting any exercise routine—large or small—it's important to ease into it. Build up your workout duration and intensity slowly over time. Doing too much too soon will leave you feeling exhausted and can lead to burnout or even injury.

THE GET FIT CHECKLIST: Think it takes a lot of gear to get started? Think again! The following items are really all it takes to get you off the couch.

✔ **A SHIRT AND A PAIR OF SHORTS OR PANTS THAT LET YOU MOVE.** While it's great if they're made of a fabric that wicks sweat away, they certainly don't have to be, especially when you're just starting out. The most important thing is that you can easily move in them and feel comfortable.

✔ **A GOOD PAIR OF WORKOUT SHOES.** Shoes are the one thing we'll tell you to splurge on because your feet need the support. A pair of cross-trainers is your best bet because they're designed for different types of activities. (Unless you only plan to run, in which case go for running shoes.) Hit up your local shoe store, get fitted, and pick a pair that feels good. And to save cash, be sure to watch for sales. There's really no reason to spend more than $75 on workout shoes, unless you really, really want to! (Or your wealthy aunt is buying.)

✔ **A SUPPORTIVE SPORTS BRA.** Whatever your cup size, a good-quality sports bra is worth the investment. Look for sports bras that are good for high-impact activities (it'll say so on the tag), and try them on before you buy to make sure they fit properly. You want a fit that offers real support, but not so snug that you feel overly compressed or get chafing anywhere.

✔ **A WATCH.** Whether it's a stopwatch, an app on your phone that allows you to track time, or an old-school wristwatch, it's helpful to have something on hand to log your workout minutes.

✔ **A GOOD ATTITUDE.** This might be the *most* important thing you need in order to get fit. A motivated mindset helps you find extra ways to squeeze in fitness even when you're super busy, and it lets you find the fun in whatever you're doing. By being committed to making yourself the best you can be, you'll find that getting fit is empowering—not dreadful.

Real Teen **TIP**

The One Thing I Need:

"A pair of dumbbells. There are so many exercises you can do with dumbbells whenever you're rushing and barely have time to exercise. I have different 20-minute workout routines I can squeeze in during the day."

— *Lina Padilla, 17, Guatemala City, Guatemala*

CHAPTER 3

Eating well

While working out is crucial to having a fit body, there's another piece to the healthy puzzle: nutrition. Eating the right foods most of the time (there's always room for a few splurges now and then) not only helps fuel your body for workouts, but it also gives you the energy you need to study, play sports, and even just laugh on the phone with your friends. The right diet can help make your skin glow and keep your hair looking shiny and healthy. Good nutrition can even help prevent you from getting colds, the flu, and lots of other annoying illnesses.

What Is a Healthy Diet?

We know that there's a ton of conflicting info out there when it comes to food. One day it's raw food; the next day it's the Zone Diet. It's enough to drive a girl crazy. Basically, you're in good shape if you eat foods that are fresh and natural, and that don't have an ingredient list filled with stuff you can't pronounce. If you can easily trace a food back to its original source—apples, for example, come from an orchard—it's likely pretty good for you. If you can't figure out where a food came from—what's the natural habitat for a Twinkie?—then it's probably a food you shouldn't eat every day.

You probably already know that whole grains, lean meats, fruits, and veggies are better for you than burgers, fries, and milkshakes. One easy eating plan to follow is the USDA's MyPlate guide. MyPlate divides meals into five major food groups: grains, vegetables, fruit, dairy, and protein. Here's the basic idea: when you sit down to eat, your plate should be about half-full of fruits and veggies, a quarter filled with whole-grains (like wheat bread or brown rice), and another quarter filled with proteins like beans, meat, seafood, or nuts. Then, as either a

PITFALL TO AVOID:
FAD DIETS

From the baby food diet to juice fasting and the Master Cleanse, there are tons of crash diets out there. All of them promise huge weight-loss and many even have celebrities who swear by them. We're here to tell you though that fad diets are NOT worth it. Not only is most of the weight you lose on them water that'll come back as soon as you go back to your usual eats, but they can also leave you feeling tired, irritable, and so hungry that even cafeteria food sounds good. Doesn't sound very appetizing, does it? Most fad diets don't have the calories, vitamins, or minerals to support your body or your lifestyle, so leave them to the infomercial stars.

healthy a food is, it's important to read nutritional labels and stick to serving sizes. Instead of eating on an oversized dinner plate, try eating off a smaller dish for dinner (encourage your parents to do the same!) and sit down to eat without any distractions. You might think you're being efficient by multitasking, but you may not realize when you're full if you're distracted. And when someone at the drive-through asks if you'd like that super-sized? Just say no!

Drink Up

Your body needs a steady supply of water to keep it functioning at its best. Your body just can't flush waste, regulate its temperature, or, you know, live, for very long without it. Without H_2O, you'll start to get dehydrated—you'll feel thirsty, hit the bathroom less, notice darker urine when you do go, and you may experience dry mouth and dizziness. You should always keep plenty of fluids on hand—but that's especially important when it's hot outside or when you're being really active.

drink, dessert, or side, you should have a serving of dairy, like frozen yogurt, low-fat milk, or cheese.

In addition to *what* you eat, you should also pay attention to *how much* you eat. No matter how

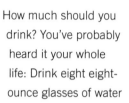

How much should you drink? You've probably heard it your whole life: Drink eight eight-ounce glasses of water every day. While you can use that as a general guideline, you don't have to be a perfectionist and measure every ounce. It's better to just keep a water bottle on hand at all times and chug often. Watch your urine output—it should be fairly frequent and the color should be light (think lemonade, not apple juice). If you can't stomach that much water, you can also count other beverages toward your daily fluid intake. Have some juice or tea (they're better than soda!), soup, or foods with high water content, like fruits and veggies.

To Eat Organic or Not to Eat Organic: That Is the Question

There's a lot of hub-bub about organic foods these days, so you're probably wondering if you should pony up the cash to get organic foods or ask your parents to do the same. The jury is still out on if organic produce has more nutrients than nonorganic produce; however, organic foods do have fewer pesticides and food additives, and are grown by more earth-friendly means. Plus, many people swear that organic foods just taste better.

If you're on the fence as to whether to buy organic or not—or simply want to try a few fruits and veggies that are organic—follow the below Dirty Dozen and Clean 15 lists from the Environmental Working Group (who also created a great, free "dirty dozen app!). This nonprofit created a list of the 12 foods with the most pesticide residue from commercial farming—the Dirty Dozen—and the 15 foods that have the least amounts of pesticides on them—the Clean 15. When deciding what to buy, try to buy organic for the Dirty Dozen list. And feel pretty good about buying the Clean 15 nonorganic!

While it's great if you can eat organic foods, if you can't afford it or don't have access, you certainly shouldn't use it as an excuse to not eat your fruits and veggies. After all, eating nonorganic fruits and veggies is certainly better than not eating any produce at all! Also, remember that just because something is labeled as "organic," it doesn't always mean that it's healthy. Organic junk food is still junk food. So again, choose unprocessed foods as much as possible.

Dirty Dozen	Clean 15
1. Apples	1. Onions
2. Celery	2. Corn
3. Strawberries	3. Pineapple
4. Peaches	4. Avocado
5. Spinach	5. Asparagus
6. Nectarines	6. Sweet peas
7. Grapes	7. Mangoes
8. Sweet bell peppers	8. Eggplant
9. Potatoes	9. Cantaloupe
10. Blueberries	10. Kiwi
11. Lettuce	11. Cabbage
12. Kale/collard greens	12. Watermelon
	13. Sweet Potatoes
	14. Grapefruit
	15. Mushrooms

PERFECTION IS BORING

In an ideal world, we'd all eat the most nutritious foods possible for every meal, and all of those good-for-you foods would taste positively scrumptious. But let's face it: Every vegetable isn't going to be your favorite, and sometimes that piece of chocolate cake will be calling your name—and loudly. While we all want to be healthy, most of us can probably agree that a "perfect" diet is unrealistic and, frankly, no fun!

Have you ever had a server at a restaurant bring you a sizzling dish and tell you the plate was hot, and that sort of just made you want to touch it more? "Off limits" foods are kind of like that. The more you deny yourself a forbidden food, the more tempting it becomes. And when foods you love are off limits, you may go overboard and totally binge when you finally do let yourself have a taste. So have the best of both worlds. Eat nutritious, good-for-you foods most of the time—like 80 percent—and don't beat yourself up for those splurges the rest of the time. That way you'll have a healthy, balanced diet without feeling deprived.

In addition to becoming a smart consumer, listen to your body. People eat for so many reasons other than hunger—boredom, anger, sadness, frustration, fatigue, stress, or sheer habit. If you think you might hit the fridge and graze for reasons other than hunger, make it a point to listen to your body the next time you're about to munch. If you're really hungry, by all means, eat up! If it turns out you're just tired or worried about that geography exam and want a distraction, deal with that instead. Take a study break, or have a friend over to hit the books with you. It'll make you feel better than food will—and it'll be more productive than eating that second bowl of ice cream.

HOW HUNGRY ARE YOU?

It's easy to say "eat according to your hunger," but what does that really mean? Well, to make things easier, we've put together an easy chart for you to follow. On a scale of 1 to 10 with 1 being so ravenous you want to eat your arm to 10 being so stuffed you couldn't possibly eat a bite more (think Thanksgiving dinner times two!), ideally you want to eat when you're at a 3 or 4 on the scale and stop eating your meal when you're at a 7 or 8.

It takes some time and practice to eat this way, but once you do, it's a great way to be mindful of your true hunger and listen to your body. Remember, it takes about 20 minutes for your stomach to tell your brain that it's full, so slow down, chew your food, and enjoy your meal, instead of rushing through it!

EATING TO TRAIN

Make sure you eat enough food whenever you bump up your workouts. Eating the right foods before and after workouts can help you build more muscle, recover from hard workouts more quickly, and give you the fuel to really rock it out. Not to mention that when you train harder, you're naturally hungrier because of all the calories you're burning! If you're trying to lose weight, it may be tempting to eat less when you work out hard, but don't do it! Your body needs the energy. Just make sure that what you're eating is the good stuff.

So what should a teen girl eat to stay healthy and fueled? Well, you'll want to start focusing more on what you eat before and after workouts. About an hour or two before you work out, have a small snack that includes some protein and carbohydrates. Some great options are an apple with a piece of low-fat string cheese, half of a PB&J sandwich on wheat bread, or a banana with a small glass of milk.

After you work out, your muscles will be tired, and you'll have used up much of the energy your body has stored. It's important to replenish with more protein and a few carbs about 30 minutes to an hour after your workout. Eating helps repair your muscles, which will help you have a better workout the next time you exercise. So, get that second snack in! Some good post-workout snacks? A small handful of trail mix, carrots with hummus, half of a turkey sandwich, or some Greek yogurt (it has more protein and less sugar than regular yogurt, making it a great choice) with a tablespoon of granola on top.

The 411 on Supplements

We always hear people ask, "Should I take a supplement?" While only a health professional or a registered dietitian should give you specific nutrition advice, our general recommendation is that as long as you're eating a healthy and varied diet, you don't need to pop supplements. Supplements are not regulated by the FDA, so there are risks involved with taking them, not to mention that not many have been fully studied for safety or for how they interact with other supplements or drugs on the market. If, however, you do have a problem getting all of your vitamins in the course of the week, then you can certainly take a well-known brand of multivitamin every few days, just to fill in any gaps. Other than that, you're good. And do not—we repeat, do not—take weight-loss supplements. They may be tempting because they promise a quick fix for energy and weight-loss, but these can be dangerous and even deadly. So avoid them at all costs! And know that real health and real results come from everything you've been reading here in this book: eating right and moving more!

And while we're talking about fueling up for workouts, remember that it's also important to stay hydrated. Be sure to begin your workouts hydrated, and drink regularly throughout your exercise session. Water is great for shorter sessions, but if you're going longer than an hour—or working out in super hot weather—drink a sports drink of some kind that has electrolytes in it, like Gatorade or Powerade. As a general rule, it's good to drink about one cup of water at least 15 minutes before exercise, then another half to full cup every 20 minutes once you start working out. After exercise, have another cup or drink water until your urine is that pale yellow color that indicates you're hydrated. As always, every body is different, so listen to what yours is telling you!

EATING DISORDERS ARE SERIOUS BUSINESS

You've probably already learned about eating disorders in health class and on TV (man, don't get us started about how skinny and unhealthy some Hollywood stars are!), but we're going to emphasize just how serious eating disorders can be—and how deadly. Also, even having "disordered eating" habits, where you don't have a full-blown eating disorder but have obsessive thoughts or compulsive behavior about food, can lead to serious negative health consequences.

We don't want to be nags, but if you or one of your friends has signs of any of the below conditions from the National Eating Disorders Association, it's important to see a professional—stat. If you want more information or help, go to nationaleatingdisorders.org.

Anorexia Nervosa: Anorexia is characterized by self-starvation and excessive weight loss.

Symptoms

❖ Refusal to maintain body weight at or above a minimally normal weight for height, body type, age, and activity level

❖ Intense fear of weight gain or being "fat"; feeling "fat" or overweight despite dramatic weight loss

❖ Loss of menstrual periods

❖ Extreme concern with body weight and shape

Bulimia Nervosa: Bulimia is characterized by a secretive cycle of binge eating followed by purging. Bulimia includes eating large amounts of food—more than most people would eat in one meal—in short periods of time, then getting rid of the food and calories through vomiting, laxative abuse, or overexercising.

Symptoms

- Repeated episodes of bingeing and purging

- Feeling out of control during a binge and eating beyond the point of comfortable fullness

- Purging after a binge (typically by self-induced vomiting, abuse of laxatives, diet pills and/or diuretics, excessive exercise, or fasting)

- Frequent dieting

- Extreme concern with body weight and shape

Binge Eating/Compulsive Overeating: This is characterized primarily by periods of uncontrolled, impulsive, or continuous eating beyond the point of feeling comfortably full (without purging).

Symptoms

- Eating unusually large amounts of food

- Eating even when full or not hungry

- Eating rapidly during binge episodes

- Eating until uncomfortably full

- Frequently eating alone

- Feeling that eating behavior is out of control

- Feeling depressed, disgusted, ashamed, guilty, or upset about eating

- Experiencing depression and anxiety

- Feeling isolated and having difficulty talking about feelings

- Frequently dieting, possibly without weight loss

- Losing and gaining weight repeatedly (yo-yo dieting)

Too Much of a Good Thing

Wanting to be healthy is one thing, but being obsessed about only eating healthy foods is another thing entirely. In fact, a new type of disordered eating is about taking "healthy eating" to the unhealthy extreme. Orthorexia isn't widely recognized by the medical community as a full eating disorder yet, but it's something to be aware of. Characterized by an obsession to eat—and only eat—healthy foods, orthorexia fixated on improving health through diet, and those who suffer from it, may spend hours planning meals, thinking about food, and even avoiding going out to eat so that they don't have to eat "unclean" foods. Just like we've said before, all good things in moderation! So if you find yourself becoming obsessed with healthy eating or feeling "bad" for eating foods that aren't 100 percent good for you, talk to your doctor or a registered dietitian for help.

YOU ARE WHAT YOU EAT

We know it's cliché, but you really are what you eat. So when you sit down to enjoy that meal or snack, take a second to think about the food and how it'll effect your body. Will it give you energy? Make you feel heavy and tired? Will it digest well for that run after school? Make a habit of choosing foods that make you feel good—inside and out!

CHAPTER 4

Waking up to fitness

Creating a healthy morning ritual can help start your day out on the right foot. A little bit of physical activity in the morning can put you in a better mood and prime you for your first period English class. You've probably also heard that breakfast is the most important meal of the day; well, it's true! You'll start your day off with energy, and it'll even help you concentrate better.

While you can work out any time of the day, mornings are great for a few reasons. First of all, a morning workout will energize you and wake you up for the day. Second, when you exercise in the morning, it's over with, and you don't have to worry about doing it later. Plus, you have the satisfaction of knowing you started your day out healthily.

Whether you're a morning person or a night owl, it's easy to throw together a quick and healthy morning routine. Even 10 or 15 minutes of activity in the morning can help you meet your activity quota for the day—and there are so many easy options for early birds. Read on for tips to getting

active in the morning and starting your day out with a healthy meal, even if you're not *really* a morning person.

THE NIGHT BEFORE

Your first step to an awesome day starts the night before. Teens need 8.5 to 9.25 hours of sleep, so if you're not hitting those numbers, get some more z's! More sleep can help your athletic performance, cut down on depression, and generally make you feel  better overall. If you're not getting enough sleep, you might find yourself spacing out in class or, even worse, while driving. Without enough rest, it's hard to function on all cylinders. And although you might think the morning battle starts at sunrise, you really set the stage for a successful wake-up call at night. Don't ignore your homework until the morning it's due. Getting it done in the evenings will allow you to enjoy your night, and you won't have to rush to finish it up in the morning. Streamline your morning by deciding what you're going to wear the night before. And, yes, that includes your workout clothes! Get them ready so they're impossible to ignore when you wake up, and make sure they're easy to find (especially if you share a room with someone else and have to dress in the dark). You can even wear them to bed to really save time!

To help yourself get regular sleep, go to bed around the same time each night, and get up at the same time every morning. Don't pack in a lot of physical activity right before you go to bed—and don't drink too much H2O either. But don't be afraid to pamper yourself! Wind down with a warm bath, a good book, or some relaxing music after a long day.

While a lot of sleep experts will tell you to center your room around sleep, we're guessing that your bedroom is your haven—and removing your TV, computer, and cell phone (ack!) from your room probably seems pretty ridiculous. Instead of taking

such drastic steps, try turning off all electronic devices an hour or two before bed. Don't fall asleep to the TV or with your Facebook page open. And step away from that cell phone! Studies show that the more reliant teens are on their cell phones, the more likely they are to experience disrupted sleep and fatigue. Sleep is too important to be interrupted by a late-night text—especially one that's just about what your friend is wearing to school the next day!

PITFALL TO AVOID: HITTING THE SNOOZE BUTTON

The snooze button can be your worst enemy. "What's another seven minutes?" you might think. But one snooze can turn into several, and before you know it, your 30-minute head start has disappeared. The solution? Make your feet hit the floor as soon as that buzzer sounds, and get your day started right (and right away).

Real Teen
TIP

How I Wake Up Feeling Fresh:

"Going to bed early (and getting seven to eight hours of sleep) always makes me feel good, but I really encourage early morning exercise. I know waking up at 5 or 5:30 am sounds absolutely terrible, but I feel so energized after a workout. Even getting up and doing a quick 15-minute workout is better than nothing."

— *Alexa Prim, Overland Park, Kansas*

people, you probably love your sleep. Half an hour is no small chunk of change, but if you work up to it in small doses over the course of a few weeks, it's really not so bad. Set your alarm ten minutes earlier three Mondays in a row, and you'll have plenty of time for a quick morning sweat session.

Still need to make that morning wake-up call less painful? Try waking up to a favorite song that pumps you up immediately. Or turn on a light when your alarm goes off. Or try opening your eyes and just giving yourself a minute or two to stretch while in bed. Choose an exercise you love so that you'll look forward to it. If you're still struggling, you can even ask a parent to make sure you rise and shine on time.

Realistically, you're not likely to leave your cell phone on the kitchen table overnight. But if you're using it as an alarm clock, leave it on the other side of the room so that you're not tempted by it, and so that you actually have to get out of bed to shut the annoying buzzer off. Once you're up, it's much easier to resist the lure of a warm bed!

And before you get to sweating in the morning, be sure to have a quick snack and some water. Nothing too big, but just a few bites and a few sips to wake your body up and get your body working. Something like half of a banana and a small spoonful of peanut butter is perfect. Then, once your workout is through and you feel all accomplished, be sure to eat a full and healthy breakfast!

WAKE UP WITH A WORKOUT

Does getting up 30 minutes earlier sound fun? Yeah, we didn't think so. If you're like most

MYTH BUSTING!

"I could never be a morning person."

If you think your sleep-loving self could never be a morning person, think again! As long as you're getting to bed early enough and getting the right amount of z's, it shouldn't matter whether you're waking up at the crack of dawn or 10 am. It's going to take some getting used to, but keep at it and you'll be getting in those morning workouts in no time! Eventually, it will even seem normal. We promise.

BREAKFAST

You may have heard your mom or dad say that breakfast is the most important meal of the day, and even though you may want to roll your eyes at their insistence that you eat something each morning, they're right. Breakfast sets the foundation for your entire day.

In fact, breakfast is so important, it's kind of like a miracle meal for your mind. Studies show that eating breakfast can help improve your math, reading, and standardized test scores (take that, SAT and ACT!), make you more able to tolerate that long day of classes, help you get along with people (no more bickering over that team science project), and improve your memory (which could mean less time studying for that chem exam).

If that wasn't enough to sell you on the amazing benefits of breakfast, this might: Other research has shown that kids and adults who regularly eat breakfast are less likely to be overweight. So basically, getting into a healthy breakfast-eating habit now will set you up for a *lifetime* of healthy, happy fitness.

Eating a Healthy Breakfast

So what is it that makes a breakfast healthy, you ask? Well, you should think of breakfast just as you would any other meal. Follow the general eating guidelines from Chapter 3, and get some protein, fiber, healthy fats, fruits and/or veggies, and some calcium in there. Eating a healthy breakfast will give you important nutrients, vitamins, and minerals at a crucial moment in your day. And, research has even found that if your breakfast is high in fiber and low in sugar, you may actually learn better. So give your day a kick-start and get eating!

If you're someone who doesn't wake up with an appetite, don't worry. Just like it takes time to get used to an early-morning workout, you can train your body to expect and actually enjoy a morning meal. Try to eat a small dinner, and skip the snacks an hour or two before bedtime. Then, if you still wake up without the desire to eat something, be sure to at least have a glass of water (usually your body is dehydrated after a night of sleep!) and a few bites of something, like low-fat cottage cheese, a piece of toast with peanut butter, or a handful of cereal. (We're big fans of cereals with at least five grams of protein per serving!) As time goes by, your body will get used to digesting food in the morning, and you can slowly begin adding more and more food to your morning nosh until it's a regular meal. Easy!

Breakfast Foods to Avoid

Just like you wouldn't expect a candy bar to make for a healthy lunch, breakfast shouldn't be a time to eat sugary processed foods either. Unfortunately,

a lot of the breakfast foods out there are full of sugar, preservatives, and other junk—and that's just not a good way to start your day, whether you're headed off to school or just hanging out on a Saturday morning. Processed foods (including donuts, waffles drowned in syrup, and cereals that have cartoon characters for mascots) may give you extra energy at first, but you'll crash soon after, leaving you tired, hungry, and craving more sugar. Definitely not how you want to start your day!

Wake Up to Good Stuff: If you're clueless about what to make for breakfast, here is a full week's worth of ideas to get your mornings started right!

> ❧ **Monday:** Three-quarters of a cup of high-fiber cereal with one cup skim milk and half a grapefruit

> ❧ **Tuesday:** An English muffin with a piece of cheese and an egg, plus a small glass of orange juice

> ❧ **Wednesday:** Two slices of whole-wheat toast with peanut butter and jelly, plus a cup of skim milk

- **Thursday:** Two scrambled eggs mixed with a handful of fresh spinach and two tablespoons of cheddar cheese, with half of a microwaved potato topped with salsa

- **Friday:** Plain low-fat yogurt topped with berries, a little honey, a few walnuts, and a small handful of crunchy whole-grain cereal

- **Saturday:** Two whole-wheat pancakes topped with light syrup, one tablespoon of butter, and a cut-up banana, plus a glass of skim milk

- **Sunday:** Small wheat tortilla filled with two scrambled eggs, salsa, one-quarter of an avocado, and two tablespoons of mozzarella cheese

Extra Credit: Three breakfast meals you can make the night or weekend before.

You might be tempted to skip breakfast altogether or just grab something quick and easy like a chocolate-chip granola bar. But with just a little planning the night or weekend before, you can have a delicious and healthy breakfast waiting for you right when the alarm goes off!

Power smoothie. The night before, fill your blender jar with a few strawberries or blueberries, half a banana, and a cup of skim milk. Cover and place in the fridge. Then, when you wake up, just throw in a few ice cubes and blend your way to a healthy shake!

Steel-cut oatmeal. Steel-cut oatmeal is a whole grain that'll stick to your ribs because it's filled with fiber. But, it can take a while to make. So, instead of forgoing it in the morning for a few more precious z's, make a big pot of steel-cut oatmeal (following the package directions) over the weekend. Once cooled, divide into one-cup freezer-safe containers and store in the freezer. Each morning, pop one serving in the microwave for a minute or so, add some tasty toppings like jelly, nuts, or fruit, and enjoy!

Mini frittatas. Eggs are a super-powerful breakfast food! If you don't like to get the stove going in the morning, whisk together four eggs, a half-cup of milk, and a dash of salt the night before. Then evenly divide into a six-cup muffin pan coated with non-stick spray. Next, add a few tablespoons of your favorite veggie (spinach, a bell pepper, or some onion all work great) to each cup. Bake at 350 degrees for 20 minutes, and you have mini frittatas that you can grab and chow in the morning!

10 Moves, 1 Minute per Move

Early Bird Gets the Workout Worm

Getting a good morning workout doesn't have to be complicated or time consuming. In fact, this ten-minute morning workout can be done just about anywhere and only requires your own body, a good pair of workout shoes, enough room to move, and a go-get-'em attitude! For this workout, you'll be doing each move for one minute—and the warm-up and cool-down are already included. If you have more time, you can always do each move for two minutes at a time, but one minute is enough for a quick and effective workout. So grab a watch or cell phone to watch the time, and get moving!

① WALKING IN PLACE WARM-UP

- **What it is:** Nothing fancy, just a quick-hitting warm-up.

- **How to do it:** Stand tall with your shoulders pulled back and your abs drawn in and just parade in place.

- **Tip:** Bring your knees up high as you march to really get the body ready to move.

② JUMPING JACKS

- **What it is:** The old gym class standard.

- **How to do it:** Jump up, jump out, and clap your hands above your head! It's jumping jacks.

- **Tip:** Keep your head lifted and look straight ahead, not down or up at your hands.

③ IMAGINARY JUMP ROPE

- **What it is:** Ropeless rope-jumping gets your heart pumping and saves you the embarrassment of ever tripping yourself up!

- **How to do it:** Circle your wrists just as you would if you were holding a jump rope. You want your whole body to be working here.

* **Tip:** Keep your feet close together with your knees soft (never locked).

④ PUSH-UPS

* **What it is:** Push-ups are a strength exercise that work out your chest, back, backs of the arms, and core.

* **How to do it:** With your hands under your shoulders and your back flat (booty not up in the air or sagging down), lower your chest down to the ground (all the way down!), and then push back up.

* **Tip:** Beginners can do modified push-ups from the knees to make this move easier.

⑤ CRUNCHES

* **What it is:** This is the quintessential move to build ab strength!

* **How to do it:** With your hands behind your head, pull your upper-torso off the ground to "crunch" your stomach.

* **Tip:** Keep your chin off your chest, and don't let your hands pull your head up to crunch—you want your abs to do the work!

To amp up your morning workout, do all the exercises with 5 lb. weights in each hand!

⑥ SQUATS

* **What it is:** Squats are fantastic for building leg strength, especially the muscles on the front of your legs and your butt.

* **How to do it:** Stand up and pretend a chair is behind you. Lowering your booty back into the imaginary chair, bend your knees to 90 degrees. Come back up to a standing position to complete one squat.

* **Tip:** Keep your weight on your heels at all times, and don't let your knees go forward past your toes.

⑦ LUNGES

❖ **What it is:** This is another exercise to build leg strength, but it also targets the booty.

❖ **How to do it:** From a standing position, step forward so that one leg is staggered in front of the other. As you step forward, bend your front leg down to 90 degrees and come up on the toes of your back leg. Push your front leg back up to stand. Repeat on the other side.

❖ **Tip:** Keep your abs in nice and tight to control your balance, and, like the squat, don't let that front knee ever go beyond your toes.

⑧ MOUNTAIN CLIMBERS

❖ **What it is**: Although this move gets your heart rate up, it also builds coordination, agility, and core strength.

❖ **How to do it:** Starting in push-up position, jump one of your legs up to your armpit on the same side of the body. Then, at the same time, move that leg back as you jump the other leg up. Repeat, repeat, repeat!

❖ **Tip:** If these are too tough (and they can be hard), just slow down your pace and make the jump less pronounced. If you want to take it to the next level, do as many as you possibly can for a heart-pumping 60 seconds.

⑨ PLANK

◆ **What it is:** The plank is a strength move that targets just about every muscle in the body, but especially your core.

◆ **How to do it:** Get into push-up position with your back flat and your hands below your shoulders. Hold it for as long as you can.

◆ **Tip:** You may not be able to hold plank for a full minute at first, and that's okay! Take breaks by resting on your knees when you need to.

⑩ SWAN DIVES

◆ **What it is:** This is your cool down plus a little bit of flexibility to get on with your day feeling energized!

◆ **How to do it:** While taking deep breaths, circle your arms out to the side and over your head. Then slowly fold your upper torso out and

down, while you lower your arms down to your sides. Hang in a forward bend for about ten seconds. Repeat sequence until your minute is up. (And feel free to go longer if you have the time!)

◆ **Tip:** Don't worry about how far you can reach down. Listen to your body and just bend forward until you feel some real tension.

CHAPTER 5

Being fit at school

With an already packed daily schedule, you might wonder how it's possible to fit in exercise, too. But if you think that your only opportunities for sneaking in a workout are before or after school, think again! Whether it's adding in an extra walk between classes, signing up for gym class, or grabbing turkey on whole grain instead of pizza during lunch, making good, healthy decisions at school can really pump up your fitness level and keep you feeling great.

Real Teen TIP

How Being Fit Helps My Grades:

"My grades are better because it's easier to concentrate when I'm under less stress. I'm more confident as my body looks and feels better when I exercise consistently. I have much more energy, and my focus is sharper when I exercise. I credit running for my high grades."

—*Isabella Judge, 16, West Des Moines, Iowa*

With so many school-approved options for fitting in activity, there's no reason for your exercise routine to become a weekend-only affair. We'll walk you through tons of awesome ways to use school-time for tone-up time, even if you think you hate P E and sports. Heck, you might even earn a few trophies along the way!

P E CLASS

In some high schools, gym class may only be required for a year or two. But if you have the option, you should consider taking gym each year—for a few different reasons. First, it's a nice break from mentally taxing classes, and you can work out that frustration during a cutthroat game of volleyball! Plus, staying active during the day is a great way to meet your daily exercise requirements. Some experts estimate that less than 20 percent of high school students are physically active in a P E class every school day for 20 minutes or more. Why not try to beat that statistic?

The advantages of P E are almost endless. Not only is it good for your physical strength, flexibility, and endurance, but it's also good for your self-confidence, stress levels, leadership skills, and even your relationships with classmates. After all, you never know when you'll bond with a new pal over your mad badminton skills! Another advantage of gym class? You get to try out tons of different activities and sports. If you're not good at one or simply hate the activity, you know you'll be moving on to a different sport in no time.

You're probably not going to be a star at *every* activity you'll encounter in P E—but you'll surprise yourself with your skills at some of them! After all, maybe you can't throw a basketball through a hoop, but your hand-eye coordination makes you a Ping-Pong pro. Maybe you can't swing a tennis racquet to save your life, but you can smoke the rest of your class in the 40-yard dash.

Afraid of participating because you have two left feet? The more activities you try, the more coordinated and balanced you'll become. Practice really does make perfect—or more perfect,

anyway! Plus, not all activities involve the same sets of skills. Activities like Frisbee golf, volleyball, and badminton require hand-eye coordination rather than strength. If coordination isn't your thing, you'll have opportunities to show off your muscles doing push-ups and rope climbing. If you're just avoiding gym because of the potential for awkward situations—picking teams, say, or sweating in front of boys—have no fear. Sure, it's not awesome if you're picked last for a team, but it's also so not the end of the world. Try to be team captain on occasion so you can do the choosing. If it's screwing up in front of boys that you're worried about, don't sweat it. Take a same-sex class and get your sweat on with the ladies if you must, but dudes can be a fun addition. Remember that, just like working out at the gym, people are more focused on themselves than on what you're doing anyway. So go for it and don't be afraid to look a little silly. If you're seriously worried about your lack of coordination, you're still not off the hook. Sign up for a weight-conditioning class for a solo daily workout experience and to learn proper lifting techniques!

MYTH BUSTING!

"I'm just not athletic."

Don't write off sports just because you don't think you have the skills. You'll never know until you try, and you can always learn! Gym class is a great way to get a taste of different activities, and you never know when you'll find a favorite that will stick with you for life. Intramural teams or non-competitive sports leagues are also a great way to try sports— with way less pressure.

GET SPORTY

If you think sports are just for the boys, think again! Research shows that there are tons of benefits for girls who participate in sports—even beyond the obvious physical and health boosts. You might think that sports will cut a huge chunk out of your study time, but girls who play sports actually perform better at school. You're more likely to graduate and do well in class than those who don't participate. This is because exercise has serious mental benefits—for learning, memory, and concentration—that can help you kick up your study game along with your ballgame. Studies also suggest that girls who play sports have higher self-esteem and better body image. Strength, confidence, and good grades? Who says girls can't have it all?

If your school is heavy on cliques, sports are also a great way to break away from that. Cliques matter less when a team is working toward the same goal, and camaraderie often takes the place of popularity contests when you're on a team. Plus, joining a sport is a great way to expand your social network and get to know girls you may never have gotten to know otherwise.

Another great thing about school sports is that there are so many options, including swimming, softball, basketball, track, cross-country, tennis, volleyball, golf, and possibly more, depending on your school. Even if your school's sports scene is super competitive, try out anyway. You'll learn a lot in tryouts, and you never know—you might even make the team!

If you're not into the time commitment a sport requires or just don't make the cut, don't give up. Less competitive options are out there! Check out your city's parks and recreation department or look into joining a YMCA league or other community program. Or grab a few friends and start an active club at school yourself; that way it can be anything you want it to be!

EXTRACURRICULAR ACTIVITIES

If you're just not that into sports, no worries. You can still get active without throwing a ball around.

Got sick moves? Try cheerleading or dance. Both activities require a high level of physical activity and hit cardio, strength, and flexibility. Not into dance but like to perform? Join the glee club. Or try the flag squad or marching band. It works the arms to hold those instruments or twirl a flag, and any marching is good for you. Not into the spotlight? Work behind the scenes for the school play, set up for school events, or make signs for the pep rally. The bottom line is to do *something fun*.

WALK ON

Walking may not seem like it's that great of a workout, but it really does make a difference. With no fancy equipment or skills needed, getting your walk on can help to lower bad cholesterol,

The Sport Possibilities Are Endless!

So many sports options, so many benefits! Whether you have an idea about what you would like to try or have no clue what sports are found in a typical school, this breakdown will help you decide which one might be for you!

Sport	Benefits	Best for
Basketball	Cardio, endurance, coordination	A team player
Cross-country	Cardio, endurance	The individual athlete
Track and field	Event dependent, but benefits include cardio, endurance, strength, coordination	Both. Relay events require a team effort, while other events are a one-girl job.
Volleyball	Leg, core, and arm strength, coordination	A team player
Softball	Sprinting, arm strength, coordination	A team player
Tennis	Cardio, total-body strength, coordination	Both. Doubles lets you play with a partner!
Soccer	Cardio, endurance, coordination	A team player
Swimming	Strength, cardio, endurance	Both. Relay events let you practice your team spirit, while individual races are your own individual pursuit.
Golf	Endurance, hand-eye coordination	The individual athlete

raise good cholesterol, decrease blood pressure, reduce the risk of diabetes, help you to stay at a healthy weight, and even perk up your mood.

And the best part is that walking is super easy to add into your routine. While getting in a solid 15- or 30-minute walk is great, a few extra steps here and there can really add up, too. If possible, try walking to school instead of driving or taking the bus. If you do have to drive, try to park farther away (or have your parents drop you off around the block) so that you have a longer trek from the parking lot to the school. Basically, think of your legs as your new form of transportation!

Strap on a Pedometer

Something as simple as a pedometer (a small step-counting device you clip on your belt) can help you to see how active you are. Just strap it on, and watch as your steps add up through the day. You don't have to spring for a super-expensive over-50-dollar model unless you want to (and have the cash). Instead, go for ones in the 20 dollar range, which are usually just as accurate and often still include bonus measurements like distance traveled, calories burned, and more.

The Real Deal on Toning Shoes

You've probably seen the ads for those fancy toning shoes that promise to deliver better results than walking in regular sneakers. But do they really work? And are they worth asking your parents for? In a word, no, they're not. Research on three popular toning-shoe brands found that they didn't give people a better workout or better results than regular running or walking shoes. And researchers have concerns that these types of shoes, which change the way you walk, may actually mess with your natural gait and could cause muscle imbalance or even injury down the line. Just another example that, when it comes to getting fit, there's no silver bullet. It's all about moving more and eating right!

10,000 Steps

For quite a few years now, many health professionals have recommended that adults walk

10,000 steps a day (roughly four to five miles) to stay healthy and active. While there are no step recommendations for teens specifically, we think 10,000 is a great number to start with. Ten thousand steps may sound like a lot, but you'd be surprised at how easily you can add more steps to your day! Besides walking to school or parking farther away, you can take the stairs whenever possible, walk back to your homeroom the long way around, or hit the track after school for a few laps. As you begin to track your steps, see how challenging it is to hit your 10,000-step target. As you get fitter and more active, up your goal to 12,000 or even 15,000 steps!

PITFALL TO AVOID: HEAVY BACKPACKS

With all of the notebooks, books, and other supplies you need for school, it's easy to feel weighed down by your backpack. In fact, backpack-related back injuries are on the rise among young people. Don't be a statistic! Limit the weight in your pack to 5 to 10 percent of your total body weight (a real-life chance to practice those math skills!) by being choosy about what you bring home and making trips to your locker more often. (Hey, it just means you take more steps!)

LUNCH HOUR

In the last chapter we stressed that breakfast is the most important meal of the day. But when you're at school, lunch is super important, too! In order to give your body and your brain the fuel they need, it's good to eat every four hours or so. This means that lunch is a priority! Eating a healthy and tasty lunch (yes, the two things can go hand in hand!) not only gives you the energy to get through that boring seventh period algebra class, it also gives your body the right nutrients and minerals—making it less likely that you'll have to eat more at night. So don't—we repeat, *don't*—skip lunch!

Skipping lunch may seem like a good idea when you need the extra time to cram for a test or when you've decided to forgo cafeteria food entirely in order to lose weight, but skipping meals is about the worst thing you can do when it comes to being healthy and fit. Missing a midday meal can leave you cranky, distracted by hunger, and feeling like a mess—which doesn't lead to good grades or good workouts. Not to mention that it'll be harder to pass up unhealthy treats in the vending machine at the end of the day. Your body needs food to support you in all that you do, so feed it right. And tell your friends to do the same!

Elements of a Healthy Lunch

Just like breakfast, you want to make sure your lunch meets the USDA's MyPlate guidelines and consists of lean protein, whole grains, dairy, and lots of fruits and veggies. It needs to be big enough to fill you up for most of the rest of the school day, but not so big that you want to take a nap an hour later. Try to fill up mainly on veggies and fruits first, and pay attention to portion sizes.

Braving School Food

Cafeteria lunch options can vary wildly from school to school. But whether your school sells mostly healthy meals or fast-food, we have a few suggestions.

- Always be sure to get a side salad or a serving of steamed veggies.

- Opt for non-fried proteins such as grilled chicken breast, baked fish, or turkey. The occasional burger even has a place in a healthy diet—but it shouldn't be an everyday lunch.

- Always go for the whole grains over the refined grains. Brown rice and whole-grain breads have more fiber and nutrients and help to fill you up longer. So skip the Wonder Bread!

- Skip the sugary drinks and juices altogether, and drink either water or low-fat milk.

- Listen to your hunger. One of the easiest ways to prevent overeating is to slow down, chew your food, and stop eating when you're about

70 percent full. It takes your brain a good 15 or 20 minutes to get the signal from your stomach that you've eaten enough, so stopping before you're stuffed is an easy way to prevent overeating.

Packing Your Own Lunch

Did you know that teens who bring their own lunches to school typically have healthier diets than those who don't? Yep, teens who brown-bag it eat less fast-food, eat more fruits and veggies, drink less soda, and eat fewer sugary and fried foods than teens who don't pack a lunch from home.

While you can buy a healthy lunch from the school cafeteria, packing your own lunch allows you to pick exactly what healthy foods you like. Also, because you're the one making it, you know exactly what's in your lunch. Bonus!

Making your own lunch doesn't have to be complicated or boring either. A wheat tortilla with some

---

Packing a Snack

If your lunch hour is early and if you have activities before and after school, you might need more than just lunch to keep your stomach from growling. If you have to go more than four hours at a time without eating (or if you always find yourself ravenous at a certain time of day), pack a snack! Whether it's a small baggie of trail mix you made at home or a lower-sugar protein bar, it's a good idea to carry a few snacks in case of emergencies. If trail mix and bars aren't your thing, try a piece of fruit and a stick of low-fat string cheese, or some beef jerky and a few baby carrots. Just like your meals, think of snacks as a way to get more delicious nutrition in!

peanut butter and jelly, along with an apple and a carton of low-fat yogurt is a tasty and easy lunch. So is a piece of leftover pizza and a side salad. Even some wheat pita or whole-grain crackers and hummus with veggies can work in a pinch!

Navigating the Vending Machine

Whether it's as a snack or as part of your lunch, the vending machines can easily be more frenemy than friend—especially if you don't know how to navigate the choices. In general, stay away from candy, chips, and the foods that are only made in factories. (Sorry, Doritos farms don't exist.) While having processed foods every now and then is fine, stick to the healthy stuff most of the time. Go for nuts, lower-sugar granola bars, or baked chips. But try not to make the vending machine a regular occurrence. Between spending your hard-earned bucks and not getting many tasty healthy options, you're much better off packing your own snacks!

Walk It Out

20 Minute Workout

If you find yourself with 20 minutes to spare, try this 20-minute workout indoors or out. You may not think that 20 minutes is enough time to get in a "good workout," but that's just not true. The key to cramming in a quick and effective workout is to compensate with some added intensity for what you lack in time.

One great way to do this is through interval training. You've probably heard of intervals before, but the basic idea is that you alternate high-intensity exercises with low-intensity exercises with no real breaks in between. You can set your intervals for however long or short you'd like (there are no hard and fast rules, really), but we like simple intervals that are easy to remember and easy to track, whether you're using a watch or a timer on your cell phone. That's why the walking workout below uses a simple formula: 1 minute at a fast pace followed by 2 minutes at a moderate pace, to be repeated until the 20 minutes are up.

When you're walking, be sure to really pump those arms, stand up straight, and get those legs moving. If you really push it during the fast intervals (and you should), you may be tempted to really slow down on your two-minute recovery interval, but try not to. The goal of the two minutes at a moderate pace is to keep your heart rate high, but let you catch your breath to the point that—in two minutes—you can kick that pace up again. As you progress and do this workout more and more, you can always swap the fast walking pace for a jog or a run!

And if 20 minutes is too much for you right now, feel free to do fewer intervals to customize this workout for youself.

WARM UP

Walk slowly for one minute. Gradually increase your pace to moderate for two more minutes.

INTERVALS

Walk as fast as you can for 1 minute, followed by 2 minutes walking at a moderate pace. Repeat this interval five times for a total of 15 minutes.

COOL DOWN

End your workout by walking slowly for two minutes to fully recover. If you have extra time, do some stretching!

WAYS TO AMP UP YOUR WALKS

Walking is a great workout, but if you want more of a challenge, why not try one of these five ways to take your walk to the next level? You can also add these options to the Walk It Out intervals for a harder workout!

- Incorporate climbing stairs or bleachers.
- Walk in hilly areas.
- Mix jogging intervals into your walks.
- Add in some push-ups or lunges.
- Keep your stomach pulled in tight to work your core and abs.

CHAPTER 6

On weekends & during the summer

After a busy school week—or school year—it's tempting to take a break and just veg out. But don't drop your healthy habits just because you're out of school. Whether it's exploring new activities that you've always wanted to try—like hiking or playing a sport—or getting an active part-time job, there are lots of fun and easy ways to incorporate more activity into your life.

You've probably got tons of daily commitments even in the summer: jobs, volunteering, chores around the house, and maybe even summer classes or college preparation. Maybe you also have a boyfriend who takes up a chunk of your time. We get it! But you can't put your workouts on the backburner just because you're busy; you've got to prioritize to get it all done. Just like you wouldn't miss a dentist appointment or an important family event, you shouldn't miss your workouts. Schedule your fitness just like you set aside time for brushing your teeth or taking a shower—and we promise workouts will be *way* easier. As long as fitness is a priority, it's easy to make time for it.

Get Fit Online

You already use Facebook, Twitter, and other social media websites to keep up with your friends, so why not use them to help you reach your fitness goals, too? Free websites such as SparkPeople.com, PeerTrainer.com, and FitDay.com let you track your workouts and even your meals and snacks to help you see where you've been and how you're progressing. Many also have a community aspect, so you can also get hot new tips from other fitness fiends!

MAKING THE MOST OF YOUR WEEKENDS AND SUMMERS

Weekends and summers give you some extra time to literally go the extra mile and do the things you can't normally squeeze into your busy weekday schedule. A little extra free time is all it takes to really kick up your fitness fun! Hit the gym to try out fun group exercise classes, or schedule a workout with a personal trainer. Walks, runs, and 5Ks can also be a blast; the enthusiasm at organized group events like these is contagious and helps keep you motivated. Plus, these events often benefit charities, so you can feel extra good about participating.

The summer is also a good time to join sports teams. Softball is the perfect summer sport to get you outside with friends. Swimming is also a quintessential summer activity. Going on a hike a little farther from home is a really fun group activity on the weekend; just be sure to pack plenty of water and a picnic or snacks to keep your energy up. Longer bike rides are also an ideal weekend pursuit. Into

Real Teen TIP

How I Stay Active During the Summer:

"I love swimming in the summer. It's a great way to cool off, and you just bring your friends along and have a really fun time."

— *Christina Gillespie, 13, Irvine, California*

adventure? Try a totally new activity! Find a zipline course in your area, take a trapeze class, or find a rock-climbing wall to pick up new skills. If you have access to a boat and a lake, waterskiing will work your entire body!

Take advantage of the weekends to prepare for the week ahead, too. Plan and shop for healthy meals and snacks, or cook a healthy meal with your family. It's a lot easier to follow a recipe when you aren't distracted by the craziness of the weekdays.

WORKING IT

If having a part-time job is a necessary part of your nights, weekends, and summers, make "work" part of your workout! So many jobs for teens require being active, so choose a job that gets you moving. Restaurant jobs—hosting and waiting tables—will add lots of walking to your day. You'd be surprised at how many miles you can walk in one shift! Stocking shelves is another way to keep moving. Painting is also a physically demanding job; school districts often hire people during the summer to paint classrooms while school isn't in session. Love kids? Babysitting is an awesomely active job. Kids are built to run around, and chasing them and playing games is a great way to stay moving. Just don't lounge around all day, watching movies and snacking!

If you love to be outside in the summer, mow lawns in your neighborhood. Pushing a mower is a cardio and strength bonanza. Cleaning pools in your neighborhood will also get you active, and maybe even earn you pool privileges! If you land in retail, don't just stand at your register when

Stay Fit During Winter Breaks, Too

The weather outside might be frightful over winter break, but don't let that stop you from being active! You may feel less inspired to get outside during the colder months, but winter has tons of unique opportunities. Whether it's shoveling your neighbor's driveway for a little extra spending money, going on that school ski trip, ice skating with your friends, or trying snowshoeing for the first time, try to break out of the indoor rut!

business is slow. Walk around and straighten aisle displays or clothing when you're bored. Not only will you get a little activity and help the time go by more quickly, but your boss will love you! Bagging groceries and bringing in carts at the supermarket are also great active ways to earn some spending money. Can't step away from sports? Get a job as a referee, or coach a little league team. If you land in the fast-food workforce, you'll be on your feet a lot, but you'll also face constant temptation from fatty, high-calorie foods. (On the other hand, it may turn out that seeing how the food is prepared could turn you off completely!) When you work at the local burger joint, it's inevitable that you'll occasionally munch while on the job. Avoid it as much as possible by eating a healthy, filling meal before your shift. Know what the healthiest menu items are for the times you absolutely *have to* eat at work. And order the small sizes—no super-sizing allowed!

If you do happen to get a sit-down office job, take breaks to walk around the office every now and then. Walk down the hall to deliver a message rather than emailing or picking up the phone. Use your lunch hour for a stroll outside or time at the office gym if there is one, and always take the stairs. No matter what job you do, wear your trusty pedometer to track your steps throughout the day!

HOW TO MAKE IT SOCIAL

When you're not working or studying, you probably just want to chill with family and friends. No need to skip a workout to do it! There are lots of ways to work fitness into your social life.

Family

Family members can be perfect workout companions. Because they live with you, it takes less planning to get an activity going! If you've got siblings, get outside and play soccer, basketball, or Frisbee. Go hiking and have a healthy picnic. Play a game of catch with your mom or throw around a football with your dad. Get your family together to do some volunteer work, too. You can help build houses for Habitat for Humanity, or pick up litter in your town.

Friends

Workouts are way more fun when you're having a good time. Plus, your friends can offer encouragement and help you stay motivated. It's harder to skip a workout when your friends show up

dressed and ready to go. Invite a few people over to try a new workout DVD. (Sharing exercise videos with your pals is a great way to keep workouts fresh and find new fitness favorites.) Go for a group jog or walk to a local park to play like kids. Get outside with a kickball tournament, a game of dodgeball, or sand volleyball. Bad weather? Stay inside to play on the Wii Fit and the Kinect, or play an old-fashioned game of Ping-Pong!

HOW TO EAT WELL DURING THE SUMMER AND WEEKENDS

While it can be easy to get into a healthy eating routine during the weekday when you're in school and generally have set times to eat, the weekends and summer have more possibilities for unhealthy eating. Whether it's a late-night pizza out with your friends, or your family's annual barbecue with all of the fixings, when it comes to healthy eating, a good philosophy is, "All things in moderation." It's unrealistic to think that you'll ever have a *perfect* diet. After all, life would be pretty sad without cake on your birthday, a burger on the Fourth of July, or stuffing at Thanksgiving. Food is such a big part of our lives and culture. You should enjoy eating! So how do you eat the foods you love and have a healthy diet at the same time? Simple: Just follow the 80/20 rule!

The 80/20 Rule

The 80/20 rule is like putting the "All things in moderation" philosophy into a formula. And even if you'd rather bang your head against a wall than do the math, we promise it's easy to follow. Just make sure that 80 percent of the food you eat

MYTH BUSTING!

"I can't afford to work out."

Working out doesn't have to cost an arm and a leg! You don't need expensive gear or gym memberships. Aside from all the active stuff you can do for free, you can also easily build a workout DVD library on the cheap. Netflix has a huge variety of exercise videos that you can get for a monthly fee. And if you have your eye on something specific, check online for tons of great used options. (Reviews on most sites will give you a good idea of what you'll be getting for your money.) Also, don't forget about your local library; you might be surprised by the selection there! Goodwill is worth checking out, too. You can also trade videos with friends to save money and keep your workouts from getting boring. If you find a DVD you know you'll love and it's not available used, ask for a new copy as a gift!

each day and week is healthy (fruits, veggies, whole grains, low-fat dairy, and lean proteins). Then the other 20 percent can be pretty much whatever you want! So if that ice cream is calling your name Friday night after the movie, enjoy it! Just get back on track with a healthy breakfast and lunch the next morning. Following the 80/20 rule is simple and works like a charm for keeping cravings fulfilled and your health in check.

Three Tips for Eating Well During Summer and the Weekends

1. **Stay Away From Junk Food, Alcohol, and Drugs:** There are certain foods that should be avoided if at all possible, even in the 20 percent of the 80/20 rule. Although you can have junk food like chips, fast-food, and candy in moderation, as you get fitter and start eating a healthier diet, you'll start to realize that these foods just make you feel blah. So unless you're really, *really* craving the stuff, hands off the junk food. And if you do eat some, keep your portions small so that they fit within that 20 percent.

Other things that you should avoid entirely are alcohol and drugs. We won't lecture you here about how bad these are for you (um, not to mention *illegal*), but try to remember that they're like the opposite of a healthy lifestyle. Instead of giving you energy and making you feel your best (which is the whole point!), they'll make you feel worse: drained, tired, and weak.

2. **Don't Cave to Peer Pressure:** We know how it can be. There's a lot of pressure to eat certain foods. Whether it's being forced to eat a second helping of Aunt Nora's peach pie or buy a candy bar for the school fundraiser, sometimes we get pressured into eating when we're not hungry or munching on foods we really don't even like that much. At the end of the day, you're old enough to make your own healthy decisions. And as long as you're eating a healthy diet most of the time (remember that 80/20 rule so that you're eating the goodies you really have a hankering for!) and following the MyPlate guidelines, you can feel confident that you are eating what's right for you.

3. **Eat Your Food, Don't Drink It:** In order to get the most out of your meals—and keep yourself at a healthy weight—it's best if you eat your calories instead of drinking them. It's super easy to chug a big soda or a sugary iced coffee or tea and then eat your regular dinner without thinking twice. Those drinks don't fill you up, and the calories can add up faster than you can say "Justin Bieber." So avoid the soda, energy drinks, sports drinks, lemonades, and other sweet drinks as much as you can. And if you really, really want them, consider them part of your 20 percent.

While 100 percent juice is a better option than some drinks, we still say eat your food and don't drink it. So instead of having OJ with breakfast, eat an actual orange. It'll give you more fiber than just the juice, and you'll fill up from it. The only beverage that this rule doesn't apply to is Mother Nature's best drink of all: water!

Is There an App for That?

These days there's an app for almost everything. But instead of using your phone to play yet another round of Angry Birds, use it to make yourself a little bit healthier. Here are five free apps worth checking out.

1. **Daily Burn.** With a sleek interface and plenty of photos, this app can help you track your workouts along with the foods you eat.

2. **Foodpics Log.** If you have trouble remembering what you last ate or don't have time to track your snacks until later, download this app; it allows you to take a photo at every meal, save it, and even add details. That way when a cupcake is calling, you can see how many carrots—or how many additional cupcakes—you've already eaten that day!

3. **MapMyWalk.** Set up a free account on MapMyWalk.com and then download this app, which will calculate how far your walk was and how fast you did it. Happy walking!

4. **Hydrate Yourself.** If you have trouble drinking enough water throughout the day, this free app tracks your water intake and gives you reminders to drink up!

5. **Nike Training Club.** We saved the best for last. This app is like having a personal trainer with you at all times. Download workouts, get rewards, and even share your workouts on Twitter and Facebook!

DANCE PARTY WORKOUT

1 to 2 Minutes per Move

You know what makes every workout just a bit more bearable? Good music! Pick out your ten favorite summer songs—five that are moderately paced but still energizing, and five other faster songs that make you want to dance—and enjoy this cardio and strength workout, which alternates fun strength-training moves with high-octane dance sessions.

SONG #1: CARDIO Play a fast party song (think "On the Floor" by J-Lo), and dance so hard that you can't sing along without taking a breath every few words.

SONG #2: STRENGTH TRAINING: DANCE FOR YOUR LIFE! Play another medium-paced song (think "Teenage Dream" by Katy Perry), grab some weights, and do the dance move from *Staying Alive.* (If you don't know what we're talking about, just Google it. At the very least, you should enjoy seeing John Travolta put on his best '70s face.)

How to do it properly:
Standing tall with your knees slightly bent and your abs in, hold a one- to five-pound dumbbell in one hand. Bring that same hand across your body, so that it's resting next to your other hand. Then, lift the dumbbell diagonally up and across your body, turning your palm upward until it's at ear height. Then press the weight straight up overhead. Repeat the move with the weight in the other hand. Keep alternating from one side to the other until the song is over.

SONG #3: CARDIO Dance along to another fast party song—one with a really thumping beat—and focus on keeping your feet moving.

SONG #4: STRENGTH TRAINING: KICK IT Play a medium-paced song again, and then use this standing lunge exercise to work your upper and lower body at the same time!

How to do it properly: Get yourself in a lunge position and hold it. With a one- to five-pound dumbbell in the same hand as your back leg, lean forward and bend your arm, tucking your elbow into your body. Then press, or "kick" your arm out and back so that it's straightened and parallel to the ground. Repeat ten times. Then switch to the other leg and arm. Keep going from side to side until the song is over.

Tip: To make sure that you're working both your upper and lower body, be sure to keep that lunge low, with your front leg at a 90-degree angle.

SONG #5: CARDIO Dance along to another fast party song, and now that you're starting to feel the burn, use that as an excuse to incorporate—or create—some new freestyle moves.

SONG #6: STRENGTH TRAINING: DROP IT LOW

Here's another two-for-one routine for your next moderately paced song. As soon as the dance track ends, it's time to "drop it low" and combine squats with a set of bicep curls. (And don't take any time off, either!)

How to do it properly: Pretend you have a chair behind you, and bend down into a low squat where your legs are bent at 90 degrees, and your knees aren't going beyond your toes. As you're squatting, do bicep curls with one- to five-pound weights, rotating your palms to face your chest as you lift. Stand up as you release your arms back down to your sides. Repeat until the song is over.

Tip: For extra toning, be sure to squeeze that bicep muscle as you bring the weights up.

SONG #7: CARDIO Dance along to another fast party song. (Try the running man for an extra shot of energy when you start to fade.)

SONG #8: STRENGTH TRAINING: PUMP IT UP For the next slow song it's time to "pump it up" with this core and back move where you hold a plank position while lifting dumbbells.

How to do it properly: Get yourself in plank position (on your hands and toes, like you're about to do a push-up) with your hands holding one- to five-pound dumbbells. Bring one dumbbell up, driving your elbow straight up and along your body. Then bring your weighted hand back into the plank. Repeat on the other side, and continue that series until the song is over. And remember, in order to really work your back, be sure to squeeze those shoulder blades together. If plank is too hard to do on your toes, you can drop to your knees. Just be sure to keep those abs in at all times. Good form is key!

SONG #9: CARDIO Dance along to another fast party song—something that sounds triumphant, because when this workout is over, you'll feel like a champ.

SONG #10 COOL DOWN Play a slower song (think "Good Life" by One Republic) and dance slowly until your heart rate begins to slow down. Then do some light stretching. Stretching at the end of a workout not only helps you cool down, but also improves your flexibility.

How to do it properly: From a standing position, slowly bend forward, trying to touch your hands to the ground. (If you can't, that's totally fine! Grab your shins or knees instead.) Hold here for 20 seconds. Then, take your legs slightly wider than hip-distance apart. Reach down to your left leg. Hold for 20 seconds. Do the same on the right leg. Go back to the center and hold for another 20 seconds. Then slowly roll up until you're standing. Repeat this entire stretching series until the song is over.

Tip: If a particular area of your body feels tight or your heart rate is super high, feel free to play two or even three songs here to give yourself plenty of time to cool down!

CHAPTER 7

Next-level fitness

Now that you know how to fit fitness into all times of the day, week, and year, there's no doubt that you're feeling more energetic and stronger than ever. But if you've gotten hooked on workouts and actually want to pump up the jam a bit more, there are so many ways to take exercise to the next level.

Working out more often and at a higher intensity can have great benefits for your health, including strengthening your heart, improving your endurance, and making your muscles stronger. Upping your distance and setting your sights on a more ambitious goal, like training for a 5K run or another competitive event, will also spur you to next-level fitness status. A little competition, guidance from a trainer, taking group exercise classes, or even a gym membership can push your workouts—and fitness—to new heights.

When you do start to train more intensely, you'll also need to pay more attention to your nutrition, and possibly eat more. You likely won't need to eat the amount of calories an Olympic swimmer may eat, but if you're training hard, make sure you're fueling up for those tougher challenges! Sites like Active.com can help you determine how many calories you need based on your level of activity. If you think you're ready to push yourself just a little bit further—taking the plunge instead of just dipping your toes in the workout waters—read on!

SETTING GOALS

Goals are super important whether you're a workout newbie or a gym rat. After all, how do you know you're improving if you don't set a goal? Think of goals as mile markers on your road to health and wellness. Each mile gets you just a little closer to your end goal: a healthier, fitter you! (Unfortunately when it comes to fitness, you're never "done.") Setting goals will keep you moving forward, instead of getting stuck in a rut.

Meeting a goal is like checking an item off your to-do list. It's just so satisfying! Plus, if you only do the same two-mile walk every day, you won't be improving after a while. You may have heard about plateaus when it comes to weight loss and working out, and it's true: Your body will adapt to the same workout after a while, so a workout that was once a challenge will start to feel easy. You'll start to maintain the status quo instead of progressing and getting stronger. To avoid the plateau

Real Teen TIP

How I Keep Pushing Myself:

"Just do it. I always say to myself, 'I'm going to run today! I'm going to run!' But then I later just find myself sitting on the couch. Having an exercising partner really helps me stay motivated because they can push you to do something you wouldn't do yourself. Plus, it's a lot more fun that way."

—*Brianna Barkhimer, 16, Sullivan, Ohio*

S = Specific
M = Measurable
A = Attainable
R = Realistic
T = Timely

Specific: When it comes to goal-setting, don't be vague. The more specific and defined your goals are, the easier it'll be to achieve them.

Measurable: In order to really track your goals, you need to be able to measure them. Put a number on your goals to see if you're measuring up!

Attainable: Don't set the bar so high that meeting your goal is impossible. This will only lead to disappointment. Pick goals that will make you push yourself, but that won't leave you feeling like a failure.

Realistic: Make sure the steps you have to take to meet your goal will fit into your everyday life. If you're trying to work in, say, a 10K between classes, you might need to rethink that one.

Timely: Your goals should have deadlines, just like that English essay does. Otherwise you might

zone, you'll need to switch up your workouts and really push yourself. Keep your muscles guessing with new and more challenging workouts in order to really see progress. When you meet a goal, you can then move the bar slightly higher. You'll be amazed at the difference goals can make!

Smart Goals

So how do you go about setting goals? It's easy. You just need to make sure that the goals you set are SMART: Specific, Measurable, Attainable, Realistic, and Timely.

working at the same goal for years! Give yourself time to meet your goal, but not so much time that it seems like you'll never get there; that's a total motivation killer!

Examples of SMART Versus Not-So-SMART Goals

See goal-setting in action with these three sample goals.

Goal 1

- **Not SMART:** I will run a marathon.
- **SMART:** I will run a 5K by next spring.
- **Why it works:** While a marathon is an ambitious goal, if you're just starting out, running a marathon might be biting off a bit more than you can chew. Plus, there's no deadline. Setting the realistic goal of a shorter race with plenty of time to prepare will help you succeed. And it's measurable: You either complete it or you don't!

Goal 2

- **Not SMART:** I will lose weight.
- **SMART:** I will lose five pounds in six weeks.
- **Why it works:** Losing weight is such a vague goal, and big numbers can be overwhelming if you have a lot of weight to lose. Breaking it into smaller goals will keep you motivated as you slim down. Realistic and healthy weight loss is one to two pounds per week; expecting dramatic results overnight will only make you frustrated.

Goal 3

- **Not SMART:** I will eat healthier.
- **SMART:** I will eat at least five servings of fruit and vegetables a day.
- **Why it works:** Being "healthier" is too vague to be a good goal. Putting a number on fruits and veggies is a great way to measure your progress. Other healthy eating goals include drinking less soda or skipping fast-food.

Rewards

So what do you do when you meet a goal? You reward yourself! Be creative and indulge: Buy a new magazine, a new color of nail polish, a pair of running shoes, or an accessory; get a massage or a manicure; download a new song; or have a movie night with your friends. Just try not to give yourself food-based rewards. With the 80/20 rule, you shouldn't be deprived of your faves anyway, and it's hard to focus on nutrition if you're looking at food as a reward. Plus it's fun coming up with non-food splurges every now and then. And once you've rewarded yourself, don't get lazy! Set a new goal for yourself—with an even more satisfying reward!

What should you do if you don't meet a goal? First of all, don't beat yourself up over it. Instead, take a look at why you didn't meet it and what you can do differently going forward. Was it realistic? Honestly attainable for you and your current fitness level? Was it specific enough, with a game plan? Was it a goal you really wanted to meet? Once you know why the goal didn't work, set a new one.

You should also keep in mind that the goal isn't always the end. Sometimes it's the push that will keep you moving forward—like if you fell short of a weekly run mileage total by a few miles, or you failed to run a race in the time you hoped for. Just because you haven't done it yet doesn't mean you won't get there!

JOIN A GYM

While you don't have to join a health club to get fit, it can certainly help you get to the next level. Gyms and their staff can be great resources when it comes to trying new equipment, getting expert advice, and taking group exercise classes.

When you're looking for a gym, don't just

sign up for a membership at the first one you see. Most gyms offer a free one-week pass so that you can test the waters. Go a few times during that week to see how you like it, and make sure it has what you're looking for. Is the staff friendly? Does most of the equipment work? (It's normal for machines to occasionally be out of order, but it's a red flag if many are sitting idle because they need repair.) Is the place clean? Is it open at times you can actually go? Is the location close enough that you'll go frequently? Do you feel comfortable with the other members? (You don't have to be besties with other gym-goers, but if they're all Mr. Universe contestants you may feel out of place!) If it's important that you have a snack bar available, a pool, a racquetball court, or a climbing wall, check those out, too. You don't want to sign up based on the fact that there's a pool if you wouldn't want to jump in it!

Learning to Use the Equipment

Whether you're familiar with health clubs or not, get a personal tour of the facilities when you join. Ask questions and get a feel for the equipment. You should also learn the club policies and procedures (like age restrictions—many clubs

MYTH BUSTING!

Lifting weights will bulk you up.

Do you think that pumping iron is just for the boys? Or that lifting weights will make you big and bulky? No way, ladies! As a girl, you have way less testosterone than the boys, so it's an entirely different situation. In fact, in order to "bulk up," you'd have to lift extremely heavy weights on a very regular basis, and eat as much protein as the Hulk. Yeah . . . we didn't think you were interested in doing that! Lifting weights that feel heavy to you (remember, the last repetition of every exercise you do should be challenging) a few times a week is a sure-fire way to build toned—not bulky—muscles.

Because they're denser than fat, muscles make your body *look* more toned, too. Not to mention that muscles make you stronger and better able to give the classmates a run for their money in gym class.

require members be at least 14 years old to use the equipment on their own and/or to take a short class on how to use the machines). Plus, weight and cardio machines vary, so get acquainted with the machines during the tour. Never hesitate to ask staff members about equipment, whether you've been a member for a week or a year. It's the staff's job to answer your questions and help with any problems, so don't be shy about using them as resources!

Exercise Classes

Group exercise classes can be an awesome way to get a killer workout. If you don't love working on cardio and weight machines, or even if you just want to try something different, classes can be hugely beneficial. The group vibe is almost always motivational. You might push yourself harder than you would during a workout on your own, and there's nothing like a bunch of fellow exercisers clapping and whooping it up to make you smile as you sweat. Music is also a huge part of group exercise classes, and studies have shown that people work out longer and perform better when they're listening to music.

Group exercise is also perfect if you want some personal attention from a fitness pro but don't have the cash for one-on-one sessions with a personal trainer. An instructor will help you with proper form and help you modify the workout to your own level. A good instructor will motivate and challenge you while also making class fun and accessible for everyone. The instructor can be a huge factor in whether you love a class or never want to take it again. So if the instructor just isn't your style, ditch the class and try something else!

If you just joined a gym and can't decide on a class, ask for a couple of recommendations from the front desk staff or a fellow member. Word of mouth is the best way to find a class you'll love, but don't be afraid to try something totally new, either. Read the class descriptions, but know that you might not know what you're really getting until you take the class a few times. Some classes will be almost identical from week to week, but some will mix it up regularly and be different each time you go.

To get the most out of the class, be a good student! Show up on time. If you absolutely have to leave early because of a prior commitment, tell the instructor when you'll be skipping out and hang near the back of the class. Show up to a new class early and, if you're at all apprehensive, ask the instructor or fellow exercisers what to expect. And while a group dynamic should challenge and motivate you, don't push yourself too hard. Always work to your comfort level to avoid getting hurt or exhausting yourself. If you've got specific physical limitations (like a bum knee, or if you just feel a move is too difficult for you), don't be afraid to ask for modifications. Instructors should be happy to work with you so you get the greatest benefit from the class.

Work With a Trainer

Most gyms have personal trainers, and they can be great resources if you're looking to increase your fitness level. Whether you're stuck in a workout rut or you've plateaued and are no longer seeing progress, a personal trainer is the ticket to bumping it up a notch. Sure, it's an expense, with trainers costing anywhere from 40 to 100 dollars an hour, but splurging on a few sessions (or

asking for them as a gift) can be invaluable. You can also see if your gym will bundle a few sessions in when you sign up for membership!

When you first meet a trainer, he or she will assess your fitness level and find out your goals for the sessions. Whether you're looking to tone up, train for distance, lose weight, or just get stronger, don't be shy about sharing your goals. A trainer can customize a plan that will help you achieve your own particular goals. Then the trainer will actually push you through workouts. Even though you may battle soreness from a few new moves, you'll likely see progress in the course of your weekly sessions. The trainer can also recommend workouts for you for the days you're not meeting so that you have a comprehensive plan.

The Gym Class Rundown

Included below is a list of some of the popular gym classes—but this is by no means a complete list, so check out what your gym offers, and don't be afraid to try new classes, and get out of your comfort zone!

Class	What to Expect	Benefits	What to Bring	Best for . . .
BodyPump	BodyPump is a full-body weight-lifting class set to super fun music.	Whole-body strength.	Towel, water.	A girl who finds lifting weights in the gym by herself a snooze-fest.
Boot Camp	Boot camp is typically a military-drill inspired workout with calisthenics and interval training. Variations on boot camp are endless!	Cardio and strength. Drills also benefit speed, agility, and balance.	Towel, water.	One with a short attention span; the variety of exercises will keep you from getting bored.
CrossFit	A super-advanced type of workout that involves high-intensity interval training.	Whole-body strength, along with developing explosive power, agility, and coordination.	Towel, water.	An advanced exerciser who is looking for the ultimate challenge.
Pilates	A mind-body workout that typically uses small, controlled movements to target all areas of the body, but especially the core. Lots of mat work!	Whole-body strength and flexibility, coordination, stress relief.	While gyms typically provide mats, bring your own so you know it's clean.	Those who like to dance, stretch, and not get too sweaty during a workout will find Pilates to be totally awesome.
Yoga	A practice using various poses to strengthen the body, mind, and soul.	Strength, flexibility, stress relief.	A yoga mat.	With so many types, from power yoga to Vinyasa, any type of exerciser can find a yoga class they'll love.
Zumba	A high-energy, Latin-flavored dance and toning class.	Cardio, strength.	Towel, water.	Someone who loves to bust a move.

Red Flags When Getting a Personal Trainer

Unfortunately, not every personal trainer will be the best fit for you. Keep looking until you find someone you feel comfortable with, and watch out for the below red flags. You know you're in trouble when . . .

- He's always checking himself out in a mirror instead of making sure you have proper form.
- She's more interested in showing you how to do the moves than letting you actually do them.
- He tells you that to see real results you must sign up for a year of sessions.
- You say you're about to pass out, and she tells you to push harder. (This only works on TV weight-loss shows, not real life!)
- He shows up consistently late. Need we remind you that you're busy and don't need to be kept waiting?
- She pushes supplements on you (because she makes commission from that sale).
- He only speaks in grunts.

TRAINING FOR DISTANCE

Whether you have a gym membership or not, setting a goal to train for a race is a great way to keep your exercise exciting! If you've been jogging off and on and are ready for a new challenge, running longer distances like a 5K (3.1 miles) or 10K (6.2 miles) or doing a sprint triathlon (750-meter swim, 20K bike, 5K run) can help to give your workouts a well-defined purpose. Instead of just "working out," you're actually training for an event. Whether you're looking to win in your age division or just finish the race (both are noble goals!), training for an event is a great way to keep your motivation high.

However, training for longer distances takes time, and you have to train smart in order to build your endurance, avoid injury, and actually enjoy the race. There are lots of online training plans for events of all distances, but here are a few of our top tips to get started, followed by a few of our favorite online resources for going the distance.

Long Distance Tips

1. **Start small.** Be the turtle, not the hare: Think slow, steady progress. If you've never run a mile

before, signing up for a 10K would be pretty silly. Instead, go with a 5K that you can walk/run. And give yourself plenty of time to work up to the distance you'll cover. You'll probably need at least two to three months to train for most events—maybe even more if you're running a longer race or doing a triathlon.

2. **Have the right gear.** We know you might not have a lot of cash, but if you're training for a race, it's important to make sure that you have the right gear. For jogging, simply have a good pair of fitted running shoes, along with some moisture-wicking apparel to keep you comfortable. When it comes to tri training, you'll also need running shoes, along with a swim cap, goggles, a swimsuit (ask the race's organizers what's best for the time of year you're racing), a bike, and a helmet.

3. **Do your research.** Just like you wouldn't show up to a final exam without studying, you should know what you're getting into before you enter a race. Do some online research on good beginner races in your area, and be sure to scope out the location of the race so that you can train for the specific terrain of your event. For example, you wouldn't want to train on a flat treadmill for a hilly 5K course! Also, make sure that you have the time to train for the race you're interested in. As a teen, you've got a lot going on already, and you want training to be something you enjoy—not another to-do list item that stresses you out. So don't drive yourself crazy training for a race that's coming up too quickly—there's always the next one!

4. **Listen to your body.** Although your training plan may say that you need to do one thing (like run two miles), if your body is saying otherwise, listen to it! While training plans are great to have as a guide, remember that you're doing a race to improve your overall health and enjoy being active. So if you feel sharp pain anywhere when training, definitely stop and see your doctor.

⚠ PITFALL TO AVOID: OVERTRAINING

When it comes to exercise, more isn't always better! In fact, working out too hard or doing too much too soon can result in injury. In order for your body to get stronger, it needs rest after tough workouts (so in practice that usually means you'll need to take off one to two days a week). So if your body is pooped, sore, or you just feel fatigued, swap a harder workout for a short leisurely walk or some easy yoga—or give yourself a day off from activity entirely. In fact, most training and running programs include in an off day from exercise for exactly this reason. It seems counterintuitive, but by giving your body some much needed rest, you'll actually perform better on race day!

5. **Enjoy yourself!** Training takes discipline, but keep in mind that you're doing this for you and your health. Look at training as special time for you to improve yourself. You're pursuing your goals one step at a time. And when you get to race day, treat it like a celebration. Most of the fun of doing a race is enjoying all of the hard work you've put in, so when you get to your event, enjoy every second!

Resources for Going Long

Hit up the internet for some great training plans and info—especially for you beginners out there. Here are a few sites we think are great.

- **Couch to 5K/10K:** With free plans to take you from your couch to completing your first 5K and 10K, this site is a new runner's BFF! CoolRunning.com

- **The Jeff Galloway Method:** Think to run a race you have to run it *all*? Nope! Check out this site, which uses a run/walk method for training distances of all lengths. JeffGalloway.com

- **Active:** From finding a fun race in your area to training plans to advice, this site is full of ways for you to start training and racing, whether you have your sights set on a tri, 10K, or trail running. Active.com

- **Beginner Triathlete:** If a swim, bike, and run is more your speed, this website will tell you everything you need to know about doing your first triathlon. BeginnerTriathlete.com

Sample Advanced Workout Week

Feel free to tweak this wide-ranging workout schedule to fit your busy life.
Just keep in mind that you should never do resistance training with the same body
parts two days in a row, and you should always have a rest day worked into your week.

Monday	30 minutes circuit training, 15 minutes of yoga
Tuesday	30 minutes jogging
Wednesday	30 minutes circuit training, 15 minutes of yoga
Thursday	15 minutes walking, 30-minute cardio intervals
Friday	Off day!
Saturday	60-minute fun cardio (sports, dance, group exercise class, etc.)
Sunday	60-minute easy bike ride

HIIT WORKOUTS

If you *really* want to take your fitness to the next level, consider doing a "HIIT" workout once or twice a week. HIIT stands for High Intensity Interval Training, and it's a powerful way to boost your cardiovascular fitness and increase your metabolism. While HIIT workouts are super quick and perfect for the busy teen, they're also pretty grueling. So try working out at a higher intensity for at least six months before trying them.

With HIIT workouts, you really have to push yourself—like seriously hard. Just like other interval workouts, you follow a period of super-high intensity with a shorter, lower-intensity interval to recover. While there are lots of ways to do HIIT training—1 minute hard followed by 1 minute easy or 30 seconds hard followed by 30 seconds easy—a HIIT workout should be so challenging that you can only do it for 15 to 30 minutes. If you can go longer than that, you're not working hard enough.

Professional athletes have long been using HIIT training to improve their performance on the field, but you can use it to either improve your running time or to simply get one heck of a workout. In fact, research shows that doing quick HIIT sessions may help boost your fitness even more than a longer, less intense workout. We'd say it's short and sweet, but it's really more like short and hard. That being said, the results are awesome. After doing a session or two of HIIT each week, your normal workouts will start to seem way easier.

And again, remember, as with any workout, it's important to listen to your body. If you ever feel any sharp pain or are totally exhausted, stop. Also, because HIIT is so taxing on your body, you never want to do more than two HIIT sessions a week—and always leave a couple days between HIIT sessions for your body to recover. If you think you're up for it, try the sample 30-minute HIIT workout on the pages that follow!

ADVANCED 30-MINUTE HIIT WORKOUT

20 Seconds per Move 10 Seconds of Rest

Warm-Up: Do a light jog or a fast walk for five minutes to warm up.

HIIT It: Do each of the below exercises at maximum intensity for 20 seconds, followed by 10 seconds of rest, eight times. You're focusing on one move at a time. So do 20 seconds of plyometric jumps, rest, 20 more seconds of jumps, and so on, until you complete eight sets. Then it's on to the next move. Rest for 1 minute in between the different types of exercises for a total of 20 minutes of HIIT.

PLYOMETRIC JUMPS

What it is: An advanced cardio move that builds leg strength and power.

How to do it: Lower down into a squat, then explode up, jumping as high as you can with your arms reaching up.

Tip: Make sure that your weight is back in your heels and your knees don't go past your toes. As you get tired, slow your pace down.

JUMP ROPE

What it is: This cardio exercise is great for improving agility and cardio endurance.

How to do it: With a nice and steady pace, rotate your wrists and lightly jump so that you can pass a jump rope under your feet.

Tip: You'll get better at jump roping with practice, so don't be discouraged if you can't jump for more than a few seconds without tripping over the rope. As your jumping-rope skills improve, see how many jumps you can complete in the 20 seconds.

MEDICINE BALL SLAM

What it is: This is a power-strength move that gets your heart rate up, while also working your shoulders, back, chest, and legs.

How to do it: Pick up a medicine ball (5 to 15 pounds is ideal) and bring it up and over your head. Then slam it down to the ground, squatting low to pick it back up again as quickly as you can.

Tip: While you're doing most of the lifting with your upper body, be sure to get in a nice low squat when you go to pick up the ball. Talk about a full-body move!

V-UPS

What it is: An advanced kind of sit-up that works your full core and improves your balance.

How to do it: From a lying position on the ground, raise your arms above your head. Then simultaneously bring your straight legs and arms up, so that

you come up to sit and your body forms a "V," with your hands touching your knees.

Tip: This is a freaking hard move. So if it's too challenging, feel free to bend your knees to make it a bit easier. If the move is still too hard to do, you can do full sit-ups instead.

Cool down: Two minutes of slow walking, followed by three minutes of light stretching.

Extra Credit: For even more cardio, add in two-and-a-half minutes of slow jogging between each exercise. This adds another ten minutes to your workout!

CHAPTER 8

Stress-busting techniques

n addition to exercise and good nutrition, taking time to rest and de-stress is an essential part of your health equation. Even the simplest tasks are more difficult when you're stressed out and frazzled. When you're at your wit's end, you may lose patience with your parents or snap at a close friend.

Sometimes, after a long day of school, tests, and BFF drama, you'll find your mind racing after your head hits the pillow, even when you're too tired to see straight. Seeing those minutes tick by in the wee hours of the morning while you're trying to recover is the worst. Not being able to fall asleep, even when you're exhausted and desperately need the rest, is super frustrating and only sets you up for more fatigue the next day.

If you find yourself going over math equations or worrying about a guy when you should be dreaming, use some of the tips in this chapter to help you relax and de-stress. Use daily exercise, yoga, and meditation to get you into that peaceful state of mind. That way you can get all the rest and relaxation you need to function at your peak!

Real Teen
TIP

How Exercise Helps Me De-Stress

"Running and yoga are my favorite ways to relieve stress. Yoga is so calming and relaxing, and running lets me clear my head. All forms of exercise are great for beating stress, though. For me, it is all about taking my mind off whatever is bothering me and focusing on being in the present."

—*Shannon Mulcahy, 19, York, Pennsylvania*

STRESS MANAGEMENT

As a busy teen juggling school, work, friends, and plans for the future, stress probably feels like a normal part of your week. Believe it or not, some stress can actually be good for you. It can help make you alert and give you energy, which is great when you're facing that big exam or playing in a championship game. But stress can really mess you up in the long run. Over time, you could be looking at anxiety and depression, obesity, heart disease and high blood pressure, and skin and menstrual problems.

Though stress is a part of life, knowing how to manage it can save your sanity. To-do lists and calendars can be your best friends when it comes to staying on top of your busy schedule. Whether you have a task list on your phone, a high-tech app, or an old-fashioned planner, staying organized will help you prioritize, finish those papers, and be on time for softball practice.

One life lesson to learn early is to avoid procrastinating. It's so easy to put things off when they seem overwhelming, but having only two pages of a ten-page paper done at nine o'clock the night before it's due is a sure-fire recipe for stress. Your best bet is to break up large tasks into smaller, more manageable chunks. Working on a big project every day for an hour will likely produce better work than pulling an all-nighter the night before it's due—and you'll be much more relaxed about the whole thing.

You can also plan homework sessions with friends to keep you motivated. Just like planning sweat sessions with your pals helps you stick to your workout schedule, planning study sessions helps you stay on track at school. And it helps to be able to bounce ideas off one another when you get stuck on a sample test problem. You'll thank yourself for planning ahead when all of your other classmates are stressing the day before a big paper or exam, and you're enjoying a night of must-see TV or taking a fun kickboxing class at the gym!

We've touted the benefits of exercise all throughout this book, but did we mention how awesome it is for stress relief? It's true. Fitting in fitness can relax tense muscles and improve your mood. Research has also found that exercise relieves symptoms of depression and anxiety.

If you want more stress relief options, there are several ways to get huge relaxation benefits and even pamper yourself at the same time.

Yoga

Yoga is hugely beneficial to your body and mind. Yoga improves strength, flexibility, and balance, and provides other health benefits. Some studies even show that yoga helps with everything from back pain, chronic headaches, neck aches, and upset stomach, to sleeplessness, obesity, anxiety, depression, and high blood pressure. Yoga helps you focus on your body and work with your breath. It's a mind-body experience that can help you send stress to the sidelines.

There are many types of yoga, ranging from super-gentle to vigorous and sweat-inducing, so don't be afraid to try a few until you find the one you love. Ashtanga, Hatha, and Vinyasa yoga all involve poses that flow from one to another at a fairly quick pace. These are more active types of yoga as well, which focus on strength and consistent

types of yoga, such as Iyengar, are less active and focus much more on the details of getting the postures and positions exactly right, and keeping your body in alignment throughout. And when it comes to restorative types of yoga, they tend to be quieter, focusing on on slower transitions and gentler poses where you are able to relax in each pose for an extended period of time.

But no matter which type of yoga you decide to try, the main focus is generally directed toward the breath and breathing techniques, helping practitioners to reduce stress and find a sense of balance through their physical movements. Most forms of yoga also include a meditative element, and focus on "being in the present moment," which is also a very useful skill to have when you feel stressed and overwhelmed.

Massage

People use massage for all kinds of reasons, like pain relief, injury treatment, stress reduction, and relaxation. Some experts even say that massage can improve mood. And did we mention that it just feels really good? If you have the time and money (it makes a great birthday present!), have a professional massage. There are many different types to choose from—hot stone, water therapy, Thai, deep tissue—but Swedish massage is a great pick for first-timers. (Check out our Resources page for a link to the American Massage Therapy Association for tips and to find a qualified massage therapist.) Taking an hour to pamper yourself with a massage is a great way to Zen out. You can also look around locally to find more affordable massage options. Massage training schools often offer massage on the cheap, or you may be able to get a massage through your insurance provider.

If you don't have the funds or time for professional massage, enlist a parent, sibling, or friend to rub your neck and upper back when you're stressed. Nobody around? Use a hand-held massage tool or rub your shoulders yourself.

Meditation/Deep Breathing

Like massage, meditation can be used to reduce anxiety, pain, stress, insomnia, and chronic illness, and boost overall wellness. Researchers are still learning more about how and why meditation is so good for the body, but taking deep breaths

THE FIVE-MINUTE CHOCOLATE ASSIGNMENT

It's hard not to feel rushed when you're eating at school. By the time you get your food, find your table, and sit down to eat, your lunch hour is darn near over. And the few breaks you get between class periods are barely enough to make it to and from your locker, let alone enjoy a healthy snack. But it's important to slow down and savor your food when you can; food tastes better when you're paying attention. You'll also eat less because you'll be more likely to notice when you're full (remember, it can take the stomach 15 to 20 minutes to tell the brain it's no longer hungry!). To learn how to slow down and enjoy your food, take a small piece of dark chocolate and take a full five minutes to eat it. You may think that it can't be done, but it can. Take time to smell it, really chew it, and let it melt in your mouth, small bite by small bite. It's amazing how satisfying just a small portion of food and sweet treats can be if we just slow down and *really* taste them!

can make you breathe more slowly and help your muscles relax. You don't have to make an hour-long commitment to meditate either. Meditating can be as simple as taking ten slow, deep breaths, or spending a few minutes in a quiet room trying to clear your mind. If you're a meditation newbie, check out a beginner meditation book from the library or look up guided meditations online. See our Resources list at the end of the book for more info.

SLEEP

Did you know that having the right bedtime ritual can help you fall asleep faster, improve your quality of sleep, and leave you more refreshed in the morning? It's true! And sleep is definitely something you don't want to skimp on.

A good night's rest is an essential part of your well-being. It helps your body and mind rest, repair, and process information from the day. When you don't get enough sleep, it can make you distracted, moody, stressed, and angry. Studies have also shown that skimping on sleep can make your skin break out, make you crave unhealthy foods, and make you more forgetful, thereby hurting your performance at school.

As a teen, your biological sleep patterns shift, so it's likely that during this time of your life, you may not feel like going to bed before 11 pm. This is where creating a bedtime ritual comes in. By winding down with the tips below, you'll be more relaxed and ready for sleep. Be sure to do these things for an hour or so before bed, and you'll be dreaming in no time.

Play the Right Music

High-energy music is great for workouts, but before bed you want to play something more low-key. Pop on some Coldplay or a ballad by Katy Perry. Choose music you like, but pick tracks that are calming. Also, be sure to play your music a little more quietly than usual. Remember, the goal is to relax.

Shut Off the Computer and TV an Hour Before Bed

Powering down all of your electronics an hour before bed gives you and your brain a chance to slow down. If you like to read before bed, choose a real book instead of an e-book on your iPad. It may seem strange at first, but it works.

Use Deep Breathing to Release Tension

You may have a million things running through your head when you lie down at night: homework, boy drama, parents on your case. But in order to fall asleep, you have to quiet your mind. Taking nice, long inhales and exhales helps to slow down your nervous system, pump oxygen into your cells, and calm you down. So before bed, whether you do it standing, sitting, or lying down, slow down and take five deep breaths. That's all it takes to relax, thereby helping you to fall asleep faster.

Take a Long, Hot Bath

Who doesn't like a hot bath after a tough day? A 10 to 20-minute soak in the tub is great for melting away stress and getting you and your body into a relaxed state. Whether you sit in a bubble bath reading a magazine, listening to music, or simply just "being," a nightly bath can be a fabulous way to unwind and prepare for sleep.

MYTH BUSTING!

"My body is stronger when I work it out every day."

While more is usually better when it comes to sleep, more is not better when it comes to working out. In fact, if you work out too much, your muscles can become weaker and your performance can suffer (not to mention it feels terrible and you become a cranky pants). Taking one to two days to recover every week—plus getting adequate sleep each night—is a must. Proper rest gives your body time to rebuild, rest, and get stronger!

YOGA FOR STRESS RELIEF

10 to 20 Minutes per Move

Yoga is a great way to unwind. So grab a yoga mat or a piece of carpet and try this stress-relief workout before you go to bed at night to stretch out and decompress. (Note: This workout also counts as flexibility training—bonus!)

MOUNTAIN POSE WITH DEEP BREATHING

How to do it: This yoga pose may look like you're just standing straight up, but it's much more than that. With your legs together, press your feet into the floor. Pull your belly button in as you bring your shoulder blades together in your back. Push your shoulders down away from your ears as you slightly lift your head up, bringing your chin down just slightly so that your spine is straight. Hold this

position as you do ten deep breaths, consciously moving the breath throughout your entire body.

What it does: This pose helps you to have better posture and body alignment. The deep breathing also calms the mind and body.

Tip: If your mind begins to wander and starts thinking about all the things you need to do tomorrow, just redirect it back to focusing on your breath. The more you do this pose, the more your focus will improve.

DOWNWARD-FACING DOG

How to do it: This is the quintessential yoga pose. Starting with your hands and knees on the floor, push your hips up to the ceiling, straightening your legs as much as you can. Then, pushing your shoulders away from your ears, extend your arms so that they're straight, too. Try to drive your heels down as much as is comfortable. Hold for five deep breaths.

What it does: Downward-Facing Dog is a full-body stretch that is great for the hamstrings and calves. It also works your upper-body and core as you hold the position.

Tip: Beginner and intermediate yogis probably won't be able to get their heels down on the ground, so just go as far as you can. Once you feel a point of tightness, stop there and breathe into the pose. Yoga is all about respecting your body and its boundaries.

TREE POSE

How to do it: Standing nice and tall, push your left foot into the ground as you raise your right foot up and place the bottom of your foot on the side of your left calf. Balance in this pose as you reach your arms up over your head. Hold here for five deep breaths, and then switch sides.

What it does: This yoga pose tests your balance and your focus. As you do it over time, you'll be able to hold it longer and longer without wobbling or losing your balance.

Tip: Think of your standing leg as the roots, your body as the trunk, and your arms as the limbs of a tree. Really push down into the earth and up into the sky to get a full stretch (and more challenging balance work).

CHILD'S POSE

How to do it: This pose may have "child" in its name, but it's certainly not just for kids! Sitting back on your heels, bring your forehead to the ground. Bring your arms and hands back by your heels. Simply breathe and relax for five breaths.

What it does: This pose is great for relaxing the body, and stretching out your legs and upper back.

Tip: If it's uncomfortable to sit with your heels under your booty, try widening the stance of your feet. It's also fine if you can't bring your forehead all the way to the ground. Again, do what's right for your body.

CORPSE POSE

How to do it: Act like a dead person! No, really. Lie on your back with your arms out to your sides and your palms up. Let your feet naturally turn outward. Take ten super-slow and deep breaths.

What it does: This restorative yoga pose is all about relaxation. You'll definitely want to go to sleep after this one!

Tip: Try not to "do" anything in this pose. Now is the time to completely let go and just be.

BEST RELAXING YOGA DVDS

There are so many good yoga DVDs out there! Here's a list of our five favorite DVDs that are guaranteed to chill you out. The best part? You can find most of them online for less than 15 dollars!

1. **Yoga for Stress Relief & Flexibility.** With two 30-minute workouts to choose from, this yoga DVD has just the right mix of stretching and relaxation.

2. **Shiva Rea Surf Yoga Soul.** With seven mix-and-match workout options, this video gives you a great variety of meditation exercises, flexibility, and a little toning—all with a surfer vibe that's super cool.

3. **Bob Harper's Inside Out Method***: Yoga for the Warrior.* Don't let the tough name fool you; this workout makes you feel great. It's a full hour and does incorporate some strength work, but by the end you will be in a relaxed state of bliss.

4. **AM and PM *Yoga for Beginners*.** With a 30-minute segment to do in the morning and one to do in the evening; we swear by the latter pm. workout before bed. It feels more like a reward than a workout.

5. **Rodney Yee's Daily Yoga.** A smorgasbord of yoga styles and types, this DVD features five 20-minute workouts to get you Zenned out, no matter if your body is craving standing poses, stretching, or deep breathing.

CHAPTER 9

Conclusion & resources

CONCLUSION

So there you have it. Your guide to fitting fitness into your life! Before we send you off on your merry, fit, and healthy way, we want to commend you for picking up this book. The first step to getting fit and feeling good is doing something to motivate yourself, which you've done. You now have the tools to get moving, eat right, and love yourself a little more than you did yesterday. Congrats!

Remember, working out and being fit isn't about what you *have* to do. It's about what you *get* to do. Living a healthy lifestyle isn't about depriving yourself or not being able to eat this or do that. Instead, it's about doing the things you love! So do the workouts you enjoy, and eat the healthy foods that you like to eat.

Through all of the advice, tips, and workouts we've shared with you, you now have the power to decide how you're going to fit exercise into your life. Find what works best for you and make a commitment to take care of yourself each and every day. Do this now, and you won't just be a fit teen, you'll have a lifetime of healthy years ahead of you.

You've got the tools—now get to work!

RESOURCES

Active.com
Check under the Resources tab for helpful calculators to figure out your nutritional and caloric needs, BMI, ideal weight, target heart rate, and more.

Amazon.com
Find new and used workout DVDs and other exercise equipment at affordable prices.

Amtamassage.org
The American Massage Therapy Association is a great resource for finding a qualified massage therapist and for getting tips on making the most of a massage.

BlackGirlsRun.com
Black Girls RUN! tackles the growing obesity epidemic in the African American community by encouraging African American women to make fitness and healthy living a priority.

ChooseMyPlate.gov
The US Department of Agriculture's recommendations on how to fill your plate with nutritious foods.

FitBottomedGirls.com
With reviews of workout DVDs, gear, and equipment, healthy recipes, and articles that will motivate you and keep your fitness humor alive, FBG is a go-to source for the latest in the health and fitness world.

FitDay.com
A free online journal that will help you track your foods, exercise, weight, and goals.

FitnessMagazine.com
With workouts, healthy recipes, and health and beauty info, this site can help keep your exercise routines fresh and your meals delicious.

GirlsHealth.gov

Straightforward health, nutrition, and fitness information specifically for young girls and teens.

GirlsontheRun.org

This nonprofit empowers and enhances self-esteem for girls ages 8 to 13. The in-school program helps girls train for a 3.1-mile run to encourage positive emotional, social, mental, spiritual, and physical development.

Hungry-Girl.com

By showing you lower-calorie swaps for high-calorie indulgences, Hungry Girl helps you eat what you're craving without the guilt!

MapMyRun.com

Find out the distance of your neighborhood run or see what cool running routes others are running in your town.

Moveit4.org/musicmovesme.php

Get a free music download to add to your workout playlist!

OnlineMeditation.org

With free guided meditations and online classes, this site helps the meditation newbie.

PEERTrainer.com

Journal your daily fitness and nutrition to keep yourself on track. Join a team for the nudge you need to get—and stay!—going.

Self.com

With fitness programs, workouts, food, and diet information and blogs, *Self* magazine makes being your best self fun.

SparkPeople.com

This fitness website is chock full of healthy living content and has a great community feature for support and motivation.

Shape.com

With the latest fitness news, training plans, healthy eats and drinks, and celebrity fun, *Shape* magazine will help you stay entertained while you're getting in shape.

TeenFitnessConnection.org

Teen Fitness Connection helps to connect teens to free summer gym memberships and classes.

WomensHealthMag.com

Women's Health magazine's site has you covered with workout plans, apps for your phone, health information, and food ideas.

ACKNOWLEDGMENTS

From Jenn: First and foremost, a big thank you to my business and writing partner Erin. We may be two peas in a pod, but you are truly a writing and editing rock star. I couldn't pick a better person to write a book with. Period. Second, a big thanks to my husband who is, no doubt, my rock and soul mate. Third, to my parents, my best friend Tish, and all of my friends and family, thanks for listening to me jabber on about the project and giving me the space and encouragement to write. You all keep me grounded—and smiling.

From Erin: I first have to thank my business and partner in writing crime, Jenn. I can't imagine having conquered this feat with anyone else, as no one else could have made writing a book this fun. Thanks for sharing a brain with me. Another huge thanks goes out to my husband, without whose unwavering support and kid-wrangling talents I could not have written even one page. I'd also like to thank my mom, who always encouraged my reading and writing, and my brothers, who gave me a million soccer games during which to cultivate my love of the written word.

From the both of us: Last but not least, a big shout out to the Zest Publishing team. If it wasn't for you guys, this book wouldn't exist. We cannot express enough how thrilled we are about getting this empowering info into the hands of teen girls everywhere!

ABOUT THE AUTHORS

Jennipher Walters is the CEO and co-founder of the healthy living websites FitBottomedGirls.com and FitBottomedMamas.com. A certified personal trainer, lifestyle, and weight management coach, and group exercise instructor, she also holds an MA in health journalism from the University of Minnesota and a journalism degree from the University of Missouri. Jenn regularly writes about all things fitness and wellness for various online publications, including Shape.com and SparkPeople.com. Her favorite workouts include CrossFit, running, strength training, yoga, and tennis (which she fell in love with in high school). She really wishes a book like this existed when she was a teen!

Erin Whitehead is co-founder of the healthy living websites FitBottomedGirls.com and FitBottomedMamas.com. Erin has a journalism degree from the University of Kansas and after working for construction equipment magazines has found her love for health and fitness writing. After having her daughter in 2010 and her son in early 2012, she's trying to figure out how to fit fitness into a busy schedule and enjoys sharing her experiences along the way. Her favorite workout is Zumba, even though she has two left feet.

INDEX

MORE FROM ZEST BOOKS

DON'T SIT ON THE BABY
The Ultimate Guide to Sane, Skilled, and Safe Babysitting
by Halley Bondy

THE LOOK BOOK
50 Iconic Beauties and How to Achieve Their Signature Styles
by Erkia Stalder

SKIN
The Bare Facts
by Lori Bergamotto

FASHION 101
A Crash Course in Clothing
by Erika Stalder

WHERE'S MY STUFF?
The Ultimate Teen Organizing Guide
by Samantha Moss, with Teen Organizer Lesley Schwartz